TOP TRAILS™
Los Angeles

Written by
Jerry Schad

Series edited by
Joseph Walowski

🐾 **WILDERNESS PRESS** · BERKELEY, CALIFORNIA

Top Trails Los Angeles

1st EDITION March 2004
  2nd Printing March 2005

Front Cover photos copyright © 2004 by Jerry Schad
Interior photos, except where noted, by Jerry Schad
Maps: Jerry Schad and Fineline Maps
Cover design: Frances Baca Design and Andreas Schueller
Interior design: Frances Baca Design
Production and additional design: Ben Pease, Pease Press
Book editor: Joe Walowski

ISBN 0-89997-347-7
UPC 7-19609-97347-8

Manufactured in the United States of America

Published by: **Wilderness Press**
               1200 5th Street
               Berkeley, CA 94710
               (800) 443-7227; FAX (510) 558-1696
               info@wildernesspress.com
               www.wildernesspress.com
Visit our website for a complete listing of our books and
for ordering information

Cover photos: Humboldt Lily, Cold Creek Canyon Preserve; Caspers Wilderness Park,
Orange County

SAFETY NOTICE: Although Wilderness Press and the author have made every
attempt to ensure that the information in this book is accurate at press time, they are not
responsible for any loss, damage, injury, or inconvenience that may occur to anyone while
using this book. You are responsible for your own safety and health. The fact that a trail is
described in this book does not mean that it will be safe for you. Be aware that trail conditions can change from day to day. Always check local conditions and know your own
limitations.

The Top Trails™ Series

Wilderness Press

When Wilderness Press published *Sierra North* in 1967, no other trail guide like it existed for the Sierra backcountry. The first run of 2800 copies sold out in less than two months and its success heralded the beginning of Wilderness Press. In the past 35 years, we have expanded our territories to cover California, Alaska, Hawaii, the U.S. Southwest, the Pacific Northwest, New England, Canada, and Baja California.

Wilderness Press continues to publish comprehensive, accurate, and readable outdoor books. Hikers, backpackers, kayakers, skiers, snowshoers, climbers, cyclists, and trail runners rely on Wilderness Press for accurate outdoor adventure information.

Top Trails

In its Top Trails guides, Wilderness Press has paid special attention to organization so that you can find the perfect hike each and every time. Whether you're looking for a steep trail to test yourself on or a walk in the park, a romantic waterfall or a city view, Top Trails will lead you there.

Each Top Trails guide contains trails for everyone. The trails selected provide a sampling of the best that the region has to offer. These are the "must-do" hikes, walks, runs and bike rides, with every feature of the area represented.

Every book in the Top Trails series offers:

- The Wilderness Press commitment to accuracy and reliability
- Ratings and rankings for each trail
- Distances and approximate times
- Easy-to-follow trail notes
- Maps and permit information

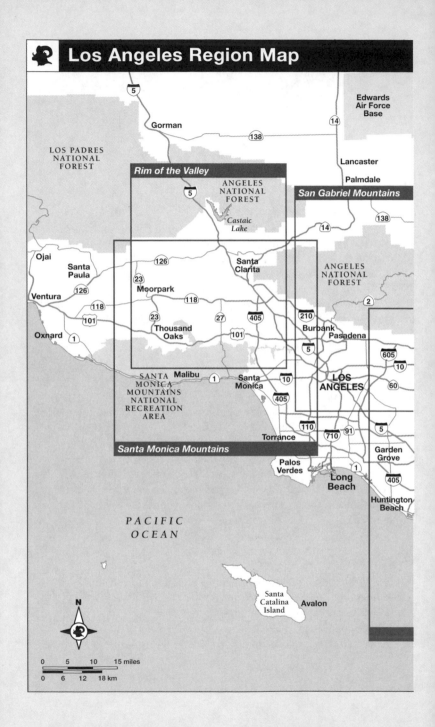

Los Angeles Region Map

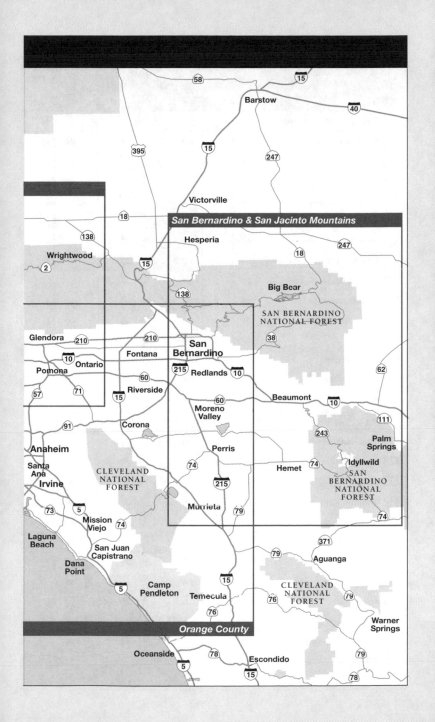

Los Angeles Region Trails

Trail Number and Name	Page	Difficulty -12345+	Length in Miles	Type	Hiking	Running	Bicycling	Permit Required	Dogs Allowed	Child Friendly
1. SANTA MONICA MOUNTAINS										
1 Mount Hollywood	27	1	3.0	↗	✓	✓			✓	✓
2 Wilacre Park	31	1	2.7	↺	✓	✓			✓	✓
3 Will Rogers Park	35	1	2.0	↺	✓	✓	✓		✓	✓
4 Temescal Canyon	39	2	2.8	↺	✓	✓				✓
5 Santa Ynez Canyon	43	2	2.6	↗	✓					✓
6 Eagle Rock	47	2	4.0	↺	✓	✓	✓			✓
7 Cold Creek Canyon Preserve	51	1	1.8	↘	✓	✓				✓
8 Bulldog-Backbone Loop	55	5	13.7	↺	✓	✓	✓			
9 Solstice Canyon	59	1	2.4	↗	✓	✓	✓		✓	✓ (wheelchair)
10 Escondido Canyon	63	2	3.4	↗	✓	✓			✓	✓
11 Point Dume	67	2	2.0+	↗	✓					✓
12 Zuma Canyon	71	4	6.6	↗	✓				✓	
13 Sandstone Peak	75	3	5.8	↺	✓	✓			✓	
14 Mugu Peak	79	3	10.8	↺	✓	✓	✓			
2. RIM OF THE VALLEY										
15 Wildwood Park	93	2	3.0	↺	✓	✓			✓	✓
16 Cheeseboro/ Palo Comado Cyns	97	3	10.3	↺	✓	✓	✓		✓	
17 Rocky Peak	101	3	5.6	↗	✓	✓	✓		✓	
18 Rice/East Canyons	105	2	3.6	↗	✓	✓			✓	✓
19 Placerita Canyon	109	2	2.4	↗	✓	✓			✓	✓
3. SAN GABRIEL MOUNTAINS										
20 Trail Canyon	123	2	3.0	↗	✓	✓		✓	✓	✓
21 Mount Lukens	127	4	8.4	↗	✓			✓	✓	
22 Arroyo Seco	131	3	10.0	↗	✓	✓	✓		✓	✓ (wheelchair)
23 Dawn Mine	135	3	5.6	↺	✓			✓	✓	
24 Mt. Lowe Historic Railway	139	4	11.4	↺	✓	✓			✓	

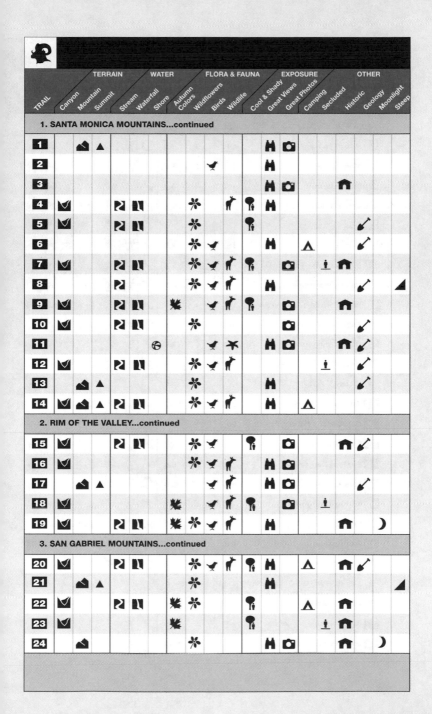

TRAIL	Canyon	Mountain	Summit	Stream	Waterfall	Shore	Autumn Colors	Wildflowers	Birds	Wildlife	Cool & Shady	Great Views	Great Photos	Camping	Secluded	Historic	Geology	Moonlight	Steep
1. SANTA MONICA MOUNTAINS...continued																			
1		●	▲									●	●						
2									●			●							
3												●	●			●			
4	●			●	●			●		●	●	●							
5	●			●	●			●			●						●		
6								●	●			●		●			●		
7	●			●	●			●		●	●		●		●	●			
8				●				●	●	●		●					●		◣
9	●			●	●		●	●	●	●	●		●			●			
10	●			●	●			●					●				●		
11						●			●	●	●	●	●			●	●		
12	●			●	●			●	●	●					●		●		
13		●	▲					●				●					●		
14	●	●	▲	●	●			●	●	●		●		●					
2. RIM OF THE VALLEY...continued																			
15	●			●	●			●	●		●		●			●	●		
16	●							●	●	●		●	●						
17		●	▲						●	●		●	●				●		
18	●						●		●	●	●		●		●				
19	●			●	●		●	●	●	●		●				●		)	
3. SAN GABRIEL MOUNTAINS...continued																			
20	●			●	●			●	●	●	●	●		●		●	●		
21		●	▲					●				●							◣
22	●			●	●		●	●			●			●		●			
23	●						●				●				●	●			
24		●						●				●	●			●		)	

TRAIL NUMBER AND NAME	Page	Difficulty 1-2345+	Length in Miles	Type	Hiking	Running	Bicycling	Permit Required	Dogs Allowed	Child Friendly
3. SAN GABRIEL MOUNTAINS...continued										
25 Hoegee's Loop	145	2	5.3	⟳	🥾	🏃		✓	🐕	
26 Monrovia Falls	149	1	1.6	↗	🥾				🐕	👪
27 Mount Lowe	153	2	3.2	↗	🥾	🏃		✓	🐕	
28 Vetter Mountain	157	1	1.4	↗	🥾	🏃	🚲	✓	🐕	👪
29 Cooper Canyon	161	2	3.0	↗	🥾	🏃		✓	🐕	👪
30 Mount Islip	165	2	5.6	↗	🥾	🏃		✓	🐕	
31 Mount Baden-Powell	169	3	7.6	↗	🥾	🏃		✓	🐕	
32 Devil's Punchbowl	173	3	6.2	↗	🥾	🏃			🐕	
33 West Fork San Gabriel River	177	3	12.6	↗	🥾	🏃	🚲	✓	🐕	👪
34 East Fork San Gabriel River	181	3	9.6	⟳	🥾	🏃		✓	🐕	
35 Cucamonga Peak	185	4	12.0	↗	🥾	🏃		✓	🐕	
36 Old Baldy	189	3	6.4	↗	🥾	🏃			🐕	
4. ORANGE COUNTY										
37 Telegraph Canyon	201	3	12.0	↗	🥾	🏃	🚲			
38 Oak Canyon Nature Center	205	1	2.0	↗	🥾	🏃				👪 ♿
39 Little Corona Coast	209	2	2.6	↗	🥾					👪
40 El Moro Canyon	213	2	6.8	↗	🥾	🏃	🚲			👪
41 Laurel Canyon	217	2	3.5	⟳	🥾	🏃				👪
42 Borrego Canyon	221	2	4.0	↗	🥾	🏃			🐕	👪
43 Main Divide	225	4	14.0	↗	🥾	🏃	🚲		🐕	♿
44 Bell Canyon	229	2	3.5	⟳	🥾	🏃				👪
45 Santa Rosa Plateau	233	2	6.0	⟳	🥾	🏃	🚲		🐕	👪
5. SAN BERNARDINO/SAN JACINTO MOUNTAINS										
46 Cougar Crest	245	3	6.6	↗	🥾	🏃		✓	🐕	👪
47 San Gorgonio Mountain	249	5	15.6	↗	🥾	🏃		✓	🐕	
48 San Jacinto Peak	255	4	11.0	↗	🥾	🏃				

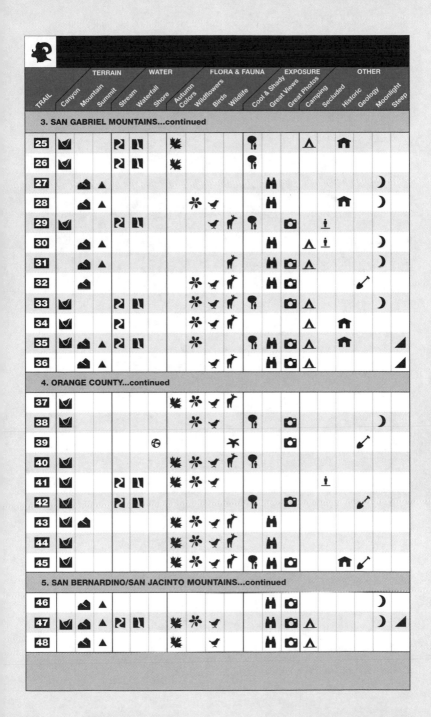

Table columns: TERRAIN (Canyon, Mountain, Summit), WATER (Stream, Waterfall, Shore), FLORA & FAUNA (Autumn Colors, Wildflowers, Birds, Wildlife), EXPOSURE (Cool & Shady, Great Views, Great Photos), OTHER (Camping, Secluded, Historic, Geology, Moonlight, Steep)

TRAIL	Canyon	Mountain	Summit	Stream	Waterfall	Shore	Autumn Colors	Wildflowers	Birds	Wildlife	Cool & Shady	Great Views	Great Photos	Camping	Secluded	Historic	Geology	Moonlight	Steep
3. SAN GABRIEL MOUNTAINS...continued																			
25	✓			✓	✓		✓				✓			✓		✓			
26	✓			✓	✓		✓				✓								
27		✓	✓									✓						✓	
28		✓	✓					✓	✓			✓				✓		✓	
29	✓			✓	✓				✓	✓	✓		✓		✓				
30		✓	✓									✓		✓	✓			✓	
31		✓	✓							✓		✓	✓	✓				✓	
32		✓						✓	✓	✓		✓	✓				✓		
33	✓			✓	✓		✓	✓	✓	✓	✓		✓	✓				✓	
34	✓			✓			✓	✓	✓	✓				✓		✓			
35	✓	✓	✓	✓	✓		✓				✓	✓	✓	✓		✓			✓
36		✓	✓						✓	✓		✓	✓	✓					✓
4. ORANGE COUNTY...continued																			
37	✓						✓	✓	✓	✓									
38	✓							✓	✓		✓		✓					✓	
39						✓				✓			✓				✓		
40	✓						✓	✓	✓	✓	✓								
41	✓			✓	✓		✓	✓	✓						✓				
42	✓			✓	✓						✓		✓				✓		
43	✓	✓					✓	✓	✓	✓		✓							
44	✓						✓	✓	✓	✓		✓							
45	✓						✓	✓	✓	✓	✓	✓	✓			✓	✓		
5. SAN BERNARDINO/SAN JACINTO MOUNTAINS...continued																			
46		✓	✓									✓	✓					✓	
47	✓	✓	✓	✓	✓		✓	✓	✓			✓	✓	✓				✓	✓
48		✓	✓				✓		✓			✓	✓	✓					

Contents

CHAPTER 2

Rim of the Valley 85

CHAPTER 3

San Gabriel Mountains 113

CHAPTER 4
Orange County 193

CHAPTER 5
San Bernardino/San Jacinto Mountains .237

Using Top Trails™

Organization of Top Trails

Top Trails is designed to make identifying the perfect trail easy and enjoyable, and to make every outing a success and a pleasure. With this book you'll find it's a snap to find the right trail, whether you're planning a major hike or just a sociable stroll with friends.

The Region

Top Trails begins with the **Region Map** (pages iv-v), displaying the entire region covered by the guide and providing a geographic overview. The map is clearly marked to show which area is covered by each chapter.

After the Regional Map comes the **Region Trail Table** (pages vi-ix), which lists every trail covered in the guide along with attributes for each trail. A quick reading of the Regional Map and the Trail Table will give a good overview of the entire region covered by the book.

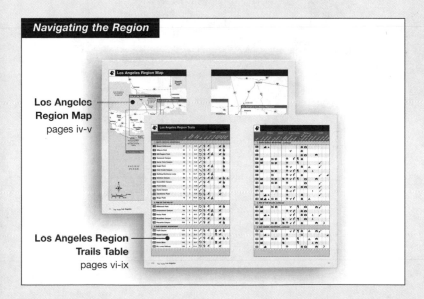

Navigating the Region

Los Angeles
Region Map
pages iv-v

Los Angeles Region
Trails Table
pages vi-ix

The Areas

The region covered in each book is divided into Areas, with each chapter corresponding to one area in the region.

Each Area chapter starts with information to help you choose and enjoy a trail every time out. Use the Table of Contents or the Regional Map to identify an area of interest, then turn to the Area Chapter to find the following:

- An Overview of the Area, including park and permit information
- An Area Map with all trails clearly marked
- A Trail Feature Table providing trail-by-trail details
- Trail Summaries, written in a lively, accessible style

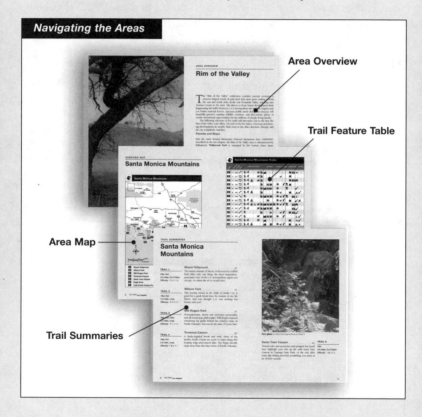

The Trails

The basic building block of the Top Trails guide is the Trail Entry. Each one is arranged to make finding and following the trail as simple as possible, with all pertinent information presented in this easy-to-follow format:

- A Trail Map
- Trail Descriptors covering difficulty, length and other essential data
- A written Trail Description
- Trail Milestones providing easy-to follow, turn-by-turn trail directions

Some Trail Descriptions offer additional information:

- An Elevation Profile
- Trail Options
- Trail Highlights
- Trail Teasers

In the margins of the Trail Entries, keep your eyes open for graphic icons that signal passages in the text.

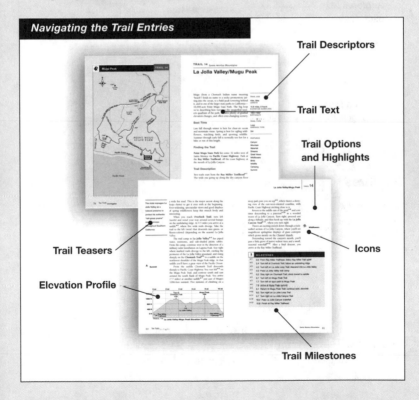

Choosing a Trail

Top Trails provides several different ways of choosing a trail, all presented in easy-to-read tables, charts, and maps.

Location

If you know in general where you want to go, Top Trails makes it easy to find the right trail in the right place. Each chapter begins with a large-scale map showing the starting point of every trail in that area.

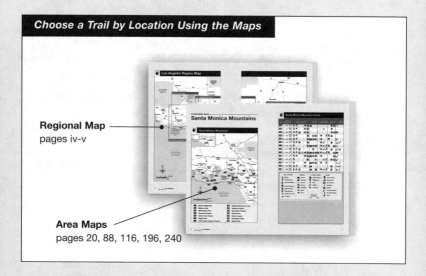

Choose a Trail by Location Using the Maps

Regional Map
pages iv-v

Area Maps
pages 20, 88, 116, 196, 240

Features

This guide describes the Top Trails of the Los Angeles region. Each trail is chosen because it offers one or more features that make it interesting. Using the trail descriptors, summaries, and tables, you can quickly examine all the trails for the features they offer, or seek a particular feature among the list of trails.

Season and Condition

Time of year and current conditions can be important factors in selecting the best trail. For example, an exposed desert trail may be a riot of color in early spring, but an oven-baked taste of hell in midsummer. Wherever relevant, Top Trails identifies the best and worst conditions for the trails you plan to hike.

Length and Elevation Change

Every trail description contains the approximate trail length and the overall elevation gain and loss. It's important to use both figures when considering a hike. The estimated time for each trail is based on this rule of thumb: allow one hour for every 2 miles, and add an hour for every 1000 feet you climb.

Difficulty

Each trail has an overall difficulty rating on a scale of 1 to 5, which takes into consideration length, elevation change, exposure, trail quality, etc., to create one (admittedly subjective) rating.

The ratings assume you are an able-bodied adult in reasonably good shape using the trail for hiking. The ratings also assume normal weather conditions—clear and dry.

Readers should make an honest assessment of their own abilities and adjust time estimates accordingly. Also, rain, snow, heat, and poor visibility can all affect the pace on even the easiest of trails.

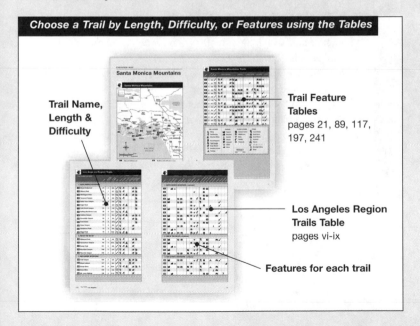

Choose a Trail by Length, Difficulty, or Features using the Tables

Trail Name, Length & Difficulty

Trail Feature Tables
pages 21, 89, 117, 197, 241

Los Angeles Region Trails Table
pages vi–ix

Features for each trail

Elevation Gain/Loss

This important measurement is often underestimated by hikers and bikers when gauging the difficulty of a trail. The Top Trails measurement accounts for all elevation change, not simply the difference between the highest and lowest points, so that rolling terrain with lots of up and down will be identifiable. It's also possible to gauge the steepness of a trail by comparing its Elevation Gain/Loss to its length.

Some Trail Entries will have an **Elevation Profile**, which provides a quick means for visualizing the topography of the route. The sample profile shows a typical trail; the elevation is in feet while the distance along the trail is in miles.

Surface Type

Each Trail Entry provides information about the surface of the trail. This is useful in determining what type of footwear or bicycle is appropriate. Surface Type should also be considered when checking the weather — on a rainy day a dirt surface can be a muddy slog; an asphalt surface might be a better choice (although asphalt can be slick when wet).

 Top Trails Difficulty Ratings (for Hiking)

1 A short trail, with little or moderate elevation gain, that can be completed in 1 hour or less.
2 A route of up to several miles, with some up and down, that can be completed in 1 to 3 hours.
3 A long, nearly flat route, or a route of short length but large elevation gain, requiring about half a day of hiking.
4 A route of both long length and large elevation change, possibly requiring a full day of hiking.
5 The most severe, both long and steep, requiring at minimum a full day's hike.

Map Legend

Trail	– – – – – – –	River	
Other Trail	– – – – –	Stream	
Freeway		Seasonal Stream	– · – · – · –
Major Road			
Minor Road		Body of Water	
Tunnel	– – – – – –	Dam	
Gate	•—•	Marsh/Swamp	ⱳ ⱳ ⱳ
Building		Park/Forest	
Bridge	)(	Boundary	– · · – · · –
Peak	▲		
Trailhead Parking	P	North Arrow	N
Picnic	⊓		
Camping	▲	Start/Finish	start & finish

Arroyo Seco's *deep canyon features cool, shady, riparian forest (Trail 22).*

Introduction

The Los Angeles region is geographically schizophrenic. The teeming world down in the Basin looks inward toward itself. The world just outside, in the hills and mountains, rises above the noise and the haze, and embraces the earth and the sky. In this outside world you will find deep-cut canyons and craggy peaks hewn in sandstone and volcanic rock (Santa Monica Mountains); bold promontories and canyon walls fashioned from shattered granitic and metamorphic rock (San Gabriel Mountains); and waterfalls, dancing streams, wooded recesses and hidden glens in places often unbelievably close to the city.

Geography

Although this book focuses primarily on the L.A-bordering Santa Monica and San Gabriel mountain ranges, selective trips are included elsewhere in the region. This book's geographic range goes as far west as eastern Ventura County and as far east as San Gorgonio Mountain and San Jacinto Peak, which are the loftiest peaks in Southern California. Coverage from north to south stretches from the Santa Clarita Valley to beyond Orange County.

Administratively, nearly all recreational areas in the San Gabriel, San Bernardino, and San Jacinto Mountains are part of either the Angeles National Forest or the San Bernardino National Forest. The Santa Monica Mountains lie in an administrative hodgepodge of county, state, and federal lands known collectively as the Santa Monica Mountains National Recreation Area. Orange County's public spaces are managed primarily by its county-parks system and (higher in the Santa Ana Mountains) by the Cleveland National Forest.

Flora

With a topographical relief of over 10,000 feet, it's not surprising that parts of the Los Angeles region could experience sub-zero winter temperatures at high elevations, and 100°F-plus temperatures in the low interior valleys. The region's varied climate, topography, and geology have, in turn, resulted in a remarkable diversity of native flora. Since many animals prefer specific habitats, the fauna of the L.A. region is also quite diverse.

Let's first take a brief, descriptive tour of the three most common plant "communities," or assemblages you will likely encounter on your back-country explorations:

The **sage-scrub (or coastal sage-scrub) community** lies mostly below 2000 feet elevation, on the south-facing slopes of the coastal mountains, and to some extent the San Gabriel Mountains. The dominant plants are small shrubs, typically California sagebrush, black sage, white sage, and California buckwheat. Two larger shrubs often present are laurel sumac and lemonade berry, which, like poison oak, are members of the sumac family. In some areas along the coast, prickly-pear cactus thrives within this community. Much of this sage-scrub vegetation is "summer-deciduous"—dormant and dead-looking during the warmer part of the year, lush green and aromatic during the cooler, wetter four to six months of the year. Wildflowers growing amid the sage scrub are particularly striking in March and April.

The **chaparral community** is commonly found between 1000 and 5000 feet elevation just about anywhere there's a slope that hasn't burned recently. Were it not for roads, firebreaks, and other interruptions, the chaparral would run in wide unbroken swaths along the flanks of most Southern California mountains. The chaparral plants are tough and intricately branched, evergreen shrubs with deep root systems that help the plants sur-

Chaparral *in the Santa Ana Mountains, Orange County (Chapter 4)*

vive during the long, hot summers. Dominant chaparral plants include chamise, scrub oak, manzanita, toyon, mountain mahogany, yucca, and various forms of ceanothus (wild lilac). Chaparral is sometimes referred to as "elfin forest"—a good description of a mature stand. Without benefit of a trail, travel through mature chaparral, which is often 15 feet high and incredibly dense all the way up from the ground, is almost impossible.

The **coniferous forest**, which has two main phases in Southern California, takes over roughly above 4000 feet elevation, at least in areas with sufficient rainfall. The "yellow-pine" phase includes conifers such as bigcone Douglas-fir, ponderosa pine, Jeffrey pine, sugar pine, incense cedar, and white fir, and forms tall, open forest. These trees are often intermixed with live oaks, California bay (bay laurel), and scattered chaparral shrubs such as manzanita and mountain mahogany. Higher than about 8000 feet, in the "lodgepole-pine" phase, lodgepole pine, white fir, and limber pine are the indicator trees. These trees, somewhat shorter and more weather-beaten than those below, exist in small, sometimes dense stands, interspersed with such shrubs as chinquapin, snowbrush, and manzanita.

Fauna

L.A.'s wildland hosts a healthy population of indigenous fauna. If you travel the trails with an observant eye, you'll eventually be rewarded by close visual contact with wild creatures.

The most numerous large creature in the region is the **mule deer**, with a population of many thousands. Deer are abundant in areas of mixed forest and scattered chaparral up in the higher mountains, and also close to the coast in the Santa Monica and Santa Ana mountains. Deer like to have a protective screen of vegetation near them at all times, and a good supply of succulent leaves to munch on, so you won't often see them in wide-open spaces.

The **mountain lion**, once hunted to near-extinction in California, has made a substantial comeback. Perhaps hundreds of these big cats roam throughout the vast mountain and desert spaces of Southern California, and a small number cling to a tenuous existence in the semi-urbanized Santa Monica Mountains. They're secretive, but wide-ranging creatures, so you're much more likely to spot the tracks of this cat than meet one face to face. Bobcats, which pose no danger unless cornered and harassed, are encountered on occasion, scampering through the canyons of the Santa Monicas or zipping across the mountain highways at night.

A few **black bears** (some of them descended from "problem bears" deported from Yosemite, and others apparently the result of gradual migration south from the Sierra Nevada) inhabit the deeper canyons of the San Gabriels. In recent years, these bears have been bothersome at several Angeles

National Forest campgrounds, where they will openly or slyly try to grab a free meal from hapless campers or their cars. Grizzly bears were once a far more serious problem in the San Gabriel and Santa Ana mountains, but they were completely exterminated by zealous hunters and settlers by a century ago.

Coyotes are universally abundant, adapting to just about any habitat (except the urban core) with ease. At the foot of the mountains, where the urban-wildland interface is often a matter of a backyard fence or the curb of a cul-de-sac, coyotes make regular forays into the suburbs to snatch small pets or obtain water and food left unattended.

Perhaps the region's most surprising large mammal is the **bighorn sheep**. About two hundred of these agile animals maintain a tough existence on the steep slopes and rocky crags of the San Gabriel Mountains. A genetically distinct subspecies roams the desert mountain ranges south of the San Jacinto Mountains. Bighorn prefer lightly vegetated, rugged terrain, on which they are capable of escaping almost any predator. They also shun contact with humans, although its not unusual to spot them near the Angeles Crest Highway. The sheep are superbly adapted to surviving on meager supplies of water and coarse vegetation.

Common mammals of the L.A. backcountry include gray fox, raccoon, and various rabbits, squirrels, woodrats, and mice. **Amphibians** include tree frogs, salamanders, and pond turtles. Several streams supporting populations of rainbow trout exist in the San Gabriels. Some are artificially stocked to meet the demand of fishermen; others are natural fisheries where catch-and-release is the only method allowed.

Reptiles include small lizards, a variety of nonpoisonous snakes, plus several species of rattlesnake. **Bird** life is varied—not only because of the coast-to-desert range of habitats, but also because the region lies along the Pacific Flyway route of spring-fall migration and also serves some overwintering birds.

When to Go

You just can't beat Southern California for year-round recreation. That being said, there definitely are optimum seasons for certain places and certain elevations within the L.A. region. Two areas covered in this book, the ocean-facing slopes of the Santa Monica Mountains and coastal Orange County, are so close to the ocean and its moderating influence on climate that they can be visited with some assurance of comfort virtually all year. The closer you are to the coastline itself, the more this is true.

Inland, the day-night variations and the seasonal variations in high and low temperatures become more extreme. Summer heat, which generally prevails from late June through early September can turn a hike in foothills

Paradise Falls in *Wildwood Park (Trail 15)*

of the San Gabriel or Santa Ana Mountains into a sweaty ordeal. But even summer days have their golden hours, right around sunrise and sunset, when the temperature hovers in a moderate register. Many of the parks and preserves in this book are closed between sunset and sunrise, so it isn't always easy or possible to enjoy these special hours of the day.

Several trails in this book ascend to high elevations where snow may cover the ground for as much as six months. It's worth noting that snow-covered trails aren't simply slower to hike; they may be dangerous due to the possibility of slipping on hard-packed snow that has turned to ice. The snow-free season for such high-elevation trails is generally May or June through November, but due to Southern California's notoriously fickle seasonal winter precipitation patterns, there are no easily definable boundaries for that season.

The rainy season, if it actually comes to pass, is normally December through March—so if it's waterfalls and lively streams you like to gaze at (or get wet in), March through May is best at the lower elevations. In the highest mountains, melting snows create plenty of runoff in April and May, but often diminish quickly after that because there is often little drainage upstream.

The wildflower bloom usually reaches a crescendo in March through May in the coastal and foothill areas. By June colorful blooms are popping out at elevations of about 5000 to 6000 feet. More subdued displays of wildflowers can be seen as high as 10,000 feet, and those might take place as late as August or even early September.

Late fall brings autumn color to the oak woodlands and wet canyons of the region. The leaves of the valley oak, black oak, and walnut turn a crispy yellow in the valleys and on the hillsides. Bigleaf maples, cottonwoods, willows and sycamores contribute similar hues to canyon bottoms spotted with red-leafed poison oak vines.

Beyond these seasonal considerations, it's worth emphasizing that nearly all the trails of Los Angeles County receive a highly variable usage depending on the day of the week. Some trails, such as those bordering Pacific Palisades or right above Pasadena, can be crowded seven days a week. Others are busy only on weekends and holidays, particularly those reachable by driving a half hour or more beyond the city's edge.

In any season, the infamous Los Angeles smog can seriously affect your enjoyment of wild areas. Strict automotive and industrial emissions controls implemented over the past three decades have resulted in dramatic improvements in the air quality; still, the Los Angeles region is noted for having some of the poorest air quality in the nation.

A good strategy for evading smog is to be aware of where it comes from and where it's going to go. Most air pollution in the region is generated in the L.A. Basin itself, where it is often confined by temperature inversions—cool marine air underlying a layer of warmer air. Try to be aware of the wind pattern, and don't go in a direction downwind from Basin-generated pollution.

Trail Selection

Three criteria were invoked during the selection of trails for this guide. First, all of the very best "classic" hikes, peak climbs, trail runs and/or mountain-bike routes around the L.A. region are included. Second, a complete range of scenery, and only the best of the types of scenery around Southern California, was included. Third, convenience is an important factor. Some highly scenic trails were excluded because access to them was long and difficult, or required rough-road driving.

With one exception, all trails in this book end at the same place they begin. While point-to-point adventures may be rewarding to those who plan well for their transportation, the logistics involved are sometimes problematical.

Key Features

Top Trails-series books contain information about "features" for each trail. Southern California, richly endowed as it is with scenery of nearly every type, has virtually every feature you could imagine—attractive beaches and rocky coastline, shady canyons, and plenty of mountains. One feature notably absent in this book, however, is lakes. Nearly every inland large body of water in Southern California is a reservoir, and almost all such bodies in the region are rimmed by roadways, or closed to public use, or not scenic enough to merit inclusion in this book.

Beautiful streams and waterfalls are a different story. In many canyons—especially in the Santa Monica and San Gabriel mountains—stream water rushes over ledges and falls sheer 10 feet to 30 feet. In a few spots, water cascades over multiple tiers with a collective drop of 200 feet or more.

If you're a first-time local hiker, you may be pleasantly surprised by the linear oases of green vegetation that snake their way through the bottoms of many of the area's larger canyons. Water flowing both on and below the surface of the canyon bottoms nourishes tall sycamores, cottonwoods, and oaks, and promotes the growth of jungle-like riparian vegetation. In many a place around L.A. you'll be amazed by the contrast between the green of the canyons and the sun-blasted, pseudo-desert landscape outside.

Wide-ranging vistas are yet another characteristic feature of nearly all L.A.-area hikes that rise to high points around the region. Peaks in Southern California aren't often smothered by tall trees or vegetation, so panoramic views are often possible.

When strong temperature inversions keep a tight lid on foggy or smoggy air below, you can rise above it all to enjoy hundred-mile visibility. Sometimes, especially in the early morning, you look down open a frothy ocean of fog that completely hides the valleys below.

Multiple Uses

Every trail detailed in this book is suitable for **hiking**, many are recommended as suitable or enjoyable for **trail running**, and a smaller number are noted as suitable (and legal) for **mountain biking**.

All trails listed are legal for running—but from the author's perspective some are so steep and difficult, or so crowded with other users (such as children), that running is impractical.

Mountain biking on trails in the San Gabriel Mountains (Angeles National Forest) is widely permitted, except on all segments of the Pacific Crest Trail. In the author's judgment, only some of the mountain-bike-legal trails in the San Gabriel Mountains are noted in this book as being suitable for mountain biking. The others—though they may be administratively classified as multi-use trails—are not recommended for mountain biking if they are excessively narrow, steep, rocky, or exposed to dangerously steep terrain.

Trail Safety

The four most common hazards found in the L.A.-area backcountry are steep, unstable terrain; icy terrain; rattlesnakes; and poison oak. Exploring

Poison Oak *can grow as a vine, as on this tree trunk, but it also grows as a shrub. Learn to recognize the stems and three-lobed leaves in all seasons.*

some parts of the San Gabriel Mountains—even by way of established trails—involves travel over crumbling rock formations on steep slopes. The erosive effects of flowing water, of wedging by roots and by ice, and of brush fires tend to pulverize such rock even further. In a single season, trails can be washed out, overgrown by thick chaparral vegetation, or blocked by fallen trees. Try to stay on the established trails, even if there may not always be specific rules preventing cross-country travel.

Again, in the San Gabriel Mountains specifically, mishaps associated with snow and ice are common. This probably happens because inexperienced lowlanders, never picturing their backyard mountains as true wilderness areas, are attracted here by the novelty of snow and the easy access by way of snow-plowed highways. Icy chutes and slopes capable of avalanching can easily trap such visitors unaware.

Rattlesnakes are fairly common in all open-space areas around L.A. below about 7000 feet in elevation. Seldom seen in either cold or very hot weather, they favor temperatures in the 75°F-90°F range—mostly spring through fall in the lower areas, and summer in the higher mountains. Most rattlesnakes are as interested in avoiding contact with you as you are with them. Be ever-vigilant, and be careful of where you put your feet and hands in the rocky areas that rattlesnakes often prefer.

Poison oak grows profusely in the bottoms and sides of canyons at elevations below 5000 feet. You'll often see it growing in semi-shady habitats, in either a bush or vine form. Learn to recognize the plant's distinctive three-leafed structure, and avoid touching any part of it with skin or clothing.

For decades, encounters with **mountain lions** (cougars or pumas) were rarely reported in Southern California. This began to change in the 1990s, due, in part, to an increase in mountain-lion population, a decrease in habitat (especially in suburban areas), and abnormal geographic displacement of deer, a prime source of food for mountain lions.

Several incidents involving mountain lions stalking or menacing campers, hikers, runners, and mountain bikers have occurred throughout Southern California in recent years. In the worst such incident, a woman was attacked and killed by a mountain lion while hiking in the Cuyamaca Mountains of San Diego County. While incidents like these are statistically rare, the following advice is worth considering:

- Hike with one or more companions.
- Keep children close at hand.
- Never run from a mountain lion. This may trigger an instinct to attack.
- Make yourself "large;" face the animal, maintain eye contact with it, shout, blow a whistle, and do not act fearful. Do anything to convince the animal that you are not its prey.

Camping and Permits

Camping opportunities abound throughout the higher mountains of the Los Angeles region: the San Gabriel, San Bernardino, and San Jacinto mountains. Almost without exception these are relatively inexpensive forest-service campgrounds that lack showers. Unfortunately, in the experience of this writer, many of these campgrounds attract a certain number of patrons who think that baying at the moon like coyotes or playing loud music until 3 A.M. is a good way to get away from it all. If you'd like to join the party, that might be fine; otherwise don't plan on getting much sleep.

Widely scattered camping opportunities can be found in the Santa Monica and Santa Ana mountains. Several state-park campgrounds in the Santa Monica Mountains offer comfortable accommodations (including showers), are fairly quiet, and require reservations far in advance for most of the year.

Only four trails in this book require wilderness permits. Full information is given for each in the respective trip writeups. Fortunately, there are no trailhead quotas for any trail listed in this book.

All trails that begin on national forest lands are subject to the National Forest Adventure pass program. This applies only to vehicles parked on national forest land, and not to users who arrive on foot or by bicycle. Adventure passes are available at all national-forest offices, ranger stations, and fire stations. They are also sold though hundreds of vendors—typically sport shops throughout the region, and gas stations and markets near the principal national-forest entry roads. Adventure passes cost $5 per day or $30 for a year. The adventure pass must be prominently displayed on your parked car—otherwise your car will likely be ticketed and fined.

On the Trail

Every outing should begin with proper preparation, which usually takes just minutes. Even the easiest trail can turn up unexpected surprises. People seldom think about getting lost or suffering an injury, but unexpected things can and do happen. Simple precautions can make the difference between a miserable outcome—or merely a good story to tell afterwards.

Use the Top Trails ratings and descriptions to determine if a particular trail is a good match with your fitness and energy level, given current conditions and time of year.

Have a Plan

Prepare and Plan

- Know your abilities and your limitations
- Leave word about your plans
- Know the area and the route

Choose Wisely The first step to enjoying any trail is to match the trail to your abilities. It's no use overestimating your experience or fitness—know your abilities and limitations, and use the Top Trails Difficulty Rating that accompanies each trail.

Leave Word About your Plans The most basic of precautions is leaving word of your intentions with family or friends. Many people will hike the backcountry their entire lives without ever relying on this safety net, but establishing this simple habit is free insurance.

It's best to leave specific information—location, trail name, intended time of travel—with a responsible person. If this is not possible or if plans change, you should still leave word. If there is a registration process, make use of it. If there is a ranger station or park office, check in.

Review the Route Before embarking on any trail, be sure to read the entire description and study the map. It isn't necessary to memorize every detail, but it is worthwhile to have a clear mental picture of the trail and the general area.

If the trail and terrain are complex, try to augment the trail guide with a topographic map; Top Trails will point out when this could be useful. Maps as well as current weather and trail condition information are often available from local ranger and park stations.

Carry the Essentials

Trail Essentials

- **Dress to keep cool but be ready for cold**
- **Plenty of water**
- **Adequate food**

Proper preparation for any type of trail use includes gathering the essential items to carry. The checklist will vary tremendously by trail and conditions.

Clothing When the weather is good, light, comfortable clothing is the obvious choice. It's easy to believe that very little spare clothing is needed, but a prepared hiker has something tucked away for any emergency from a surprise shower to an unexpected overnight in a remote area.

Clothing includes proper footwear, essential for hiking and running. As a trail becomes more demanding, you will need footwear that performs. Running shoes are fine for many trails. If you will be carrying substantial weight or encountering rugged terrain, step up to hiking boots.

In hot, sunny weather, proper clothing includes a hat, sunglasses, long-sleeved shirt and sunscreen. In cooler weather, particularly when it's wet, carry waterproof outer garments and quick-drying undergarments (avoid cotton). As general rule, whatever the conditions, bring layers that can be combined or removed to provide comfort and protection from the elements in a wide variety of conditions.

Water Never embark on a trail without carrying water. At all times, particularly in warm weather, adequate water is of key importance. Experts recommend at least two quarts of water per day, and when hiking in heat a gallon or more may be more appropriate. At the extreme, dehydration can be life threatening. More commonly, inadequate water brings fatigue and muscle aches.

For most outings, unless the day is very hot or the trail very long, you should plan to carry sufficient water for the entire trail. Unfortunately, in North America natural water sources are questionable, generally loaded with various risks: bacteria, viruses, and fertilizers.

Water Treatment If it's necessary to make use of trailside water, you should filter or treat it. There are three methods for treating water: boiling, chemical treatment, and filtering. Boiling is best, but often impractical—it requires a heat source, a pot, and time. Chemical treatments, available in sporting goods stores, handle some problems, including the troublesome Giardia parasite, but will not combat many man-made chemical pollutants. The preferred method is filtration, which removes Giardia and other contaminants and doesn't leave any unpleasant aftertaste.

If this hasn't convinced you to carry all the water you need, one final admonishment: be prepared for surprises. Water sources described in the text or on maps can change course or dry up completely. Never run your water bottle dry in expectation of the next source; fill up when water is available and always keep a little in reserve.

Food

While not as critical as water, food is energy and its importance shouldn't be underestimated. Avoid foods that are hard to digest, such as candy bars and potato chips. Carry high energy, fast-digesting foods: nutrition bars, dehydrated fruit, gorp, jerky. Bring a little extra food—it's good protection against an outing that turns unexpectedly long, perhaps due to weather or losing your way.

Less than Essential, But Useful Items

Map and Compass (*and the know-how to use them*) Many trails don't require much navigation, meaning a map and compass aren't always as essential as water or food—but it can be a close call. If the trail is remote or infrequently visited, a map and compass should be considered necessities.

A hand-held GPS (Global Positioning Satellite) receiver is also a useful trail companion, but is really no substitute for a map and compass; knowing your longitude and latitude is not much help without a map.

Cell Phone Most parts of the country, even remote destinations, have some level of cellular coverage. In extreme circumstances, a cell phone can be a lifesaver. But don't depend on it; coverage is unpredictable and batteries fail. And be sure that the occasion warrants the phone call—a blister doesn't justify a call to search and rescue.

Gear Depending on the remoteness and rigor of the trail, there are many additional useful items to consider; pocket knife, flashlight, fire source (water-proof matches, light, or flint), and a first-aid kit.

Every member of your party should carry the appropriate essential items described above; groups often split up or get separated along the trail. Solo hikers should be even more disciplined about preparation, and carry more gear. Traveling solo is inherently more risky. This isn't meant to discourage solo travel, simply to emphasize the need for extra preparation. Solo hikers should make a habit of carrying a little more gear than absolutely necessary.

Trail Etiquette

Trail Checklist

- Leave no trace
- Stay on the trail
- Share the trail
- Leave it there

The overriding rule on the trail is **Leave No Trace**. Interest in visiting natural areas continues to increase in North America, even as the quantity of unspoiled natural areas continues to shrink. These pressures make it ever more critical that we leave no trace of our visit.

Never Litter If you carried it in, it's easy enough to carry it out. Leave the trail in the same, if not better condition than you find it. Try picking up any litter you encounter and packing it out—it's a great feeling! Just one piece of garbage and you've made a difference.

Stay on the Trail Paths have been created, sometimes over many years, for many purposes: to protect the surrounding natural areas, to avoid dangers, and to provide the best route. Leaving the trail can cause damage that takes years to undo. Never cut switchbacks. Shortcutting rarely saves energy or time, and it takes a terrible toll on the land, trampling plant life and hastening erosion. Moreover, safety and consideration intersect on the trail. It's hard to get truly lost if you stay on the trail.

Share the Trail The best trails attract many visitors and you should be prepared to share the trail with others. Do your part to minimize impact. Commonly accepted trail etiquette dictates that **bike riders yield to both hikers and equestrians**, **hikers yield to horseback riders**, **downhill hikers yield to uphill hikers**, and **everyone stays to the right**. Not everyone knows these rules of the road, so let common sense and good humor be the final guide.

Leave it There Destruction or removal of plants and animals, or historical, prehistoric or geological items, is certainly unethical and almost always illegal.

Getting Lost If you become lost on the trail, stay on the trail. Stop and take stock of the situation. In many cases, a few minutes of calm reflection will yield a solution. Consider all the clues available; use the sun to identify directions if you don't have a compass. If you determine that you are indeed lost, stay on the main trail and stay put. You are more likely to encounter other people if you stay in one place.

Santa Monica Mountains

Santa Monica Mountains

The Santa Monica Mountains are a study in environmental contrast. The eastern one-fourth of the range—from Griffith Park to Interstate 405—knifes deeply into the densely populated Los Angeles Basin. Even though Griffith Park and smaller units of parkland preserve some of the original habitat, canyon-hugging and cliff-hanging residences dominate the landscape here. The central section, encompassing about half of the range's total length, rises abruptly from the coastline at Pacific Palisades and through Malibu. Two large state parks (Topanga and Malibu Creek) and numerous other parkland parcels coexist with scattered suburban and rural development. The westernmost one-fourth of the range, bordering a lonely and barely populated coastline, includes spacious Point Mugu State Park. This is the loneliest, least developed part of the range.

Throughout the Santa Monica Mountains, you'll be impressed by steep, rocky gorges, rounded hillsides, ocean vistas, and seasonal wildflower displays. More than 500 miles of hiking and multi-use trails open to the public are here, including the nearly completed Backbone Trail that will link major parks in the area. The 14 easily accessible trails listed below have been selected to maximize your enjoyment.

Permits and Maps

Nearly all public lands within the Santa Monica Mountains fall within the administrative boundary of the Santa Monica Mountains National Recreation Area (SMMNRA), a unit of the National Park Service. The SMM-NRA consists of a patchwork of public and private lands covering the Santa Monicas, plus an outlying extension into the Simi Hills to the north. For now (and perhaps for a very long time) the administration of the various park units is parceled out to several agencies, including the City of Los Angeles, the County of Los Angeles, California State Parks, the Santa Monica Mountains Conservancy (a state agency), and the National Park Service. Administrative coverage of given public parcels are subject to change, as well as the rules that govern each of those parcels.

The best single source of current information for this Balkanized park system is the National Park Service headquarters and visitor information center, 401 West Hillcrest Drive, Thousand Oaks, CA 91360. Call the visitor center at (805) 370-2301, or visit the SMMNRA website www.nps.gov/samo for more information. The visitor center itself, open 9 A.M. to 5 P.M. daily, can be reached by taking the 101 Freeway to the Lynn Road exit. Go north on Lynn Road for one block to Hillcrest Drive, and turn right. Follow Hillcrest to McCloud Avenue on the left, and follow the signs to the visitor center.

The visitor center offers books and maps for sale, plus plenty of free handouts covering the major park units administered by the National Park Service. On sale here (and from other vendors) are large-scale topographic maps of the SMMNRA published by Trails Illustrated and Tom Harrison Cartography. Maps of individual state parks are on sale as well. For most of the 14 trails described in this chapter, trail maps are available, sometimes free and sometimes for a small fee, at the trailhead or park entrance.

A free, quarterly calendar of hikes and other activities within the SMMNRA, *Outdoors, Santa Monica Mountains Recreation Area*, may obtained at the visitor center. You can apply for a free subscription to *Outdoors* for up to one year.

For many years, Griffith Park, which lies outside the SMMNRA, has lacked a decent map of its trails. A poorly drawn and photocopied free map is available from the Griffith Park ranger office on Griffith Park's east side.

For driving purposes, the Automobile Club of Southern California's *Los Angeles and Orange Counties and Vicinity* map is highly recommended for the Santa Monica Mountains and all other areas covered by this book.

National Park Service-managed units in the SMMNRA typically charge no fees, while the state and county-run parks do. Hours and fees (if any) for the various SMMNRA units will be noted in the trail descriptions below. Aside from parking or day-use fees, no other permit is required to enter public lands of the Santa Monica Mountains.

Santa Monica Mountains

Santa Monica Mountains

1	Mount Hollywood	**8**	Bulldog-Backbone Loop
2	Wilacre Park	**9**	Solstice Canyon
3	Will Rogers Park	**10**	Escondido Canyon
4	Temescal Canyon	**11**	Point Dume
5	Santa Ynez Canyon	**12**	Zuma Canyon
6	Eagle Rock	**13**	Sandstone Peak
7	Cold Creek Canyon Preserve	**14**	Mugu Peak

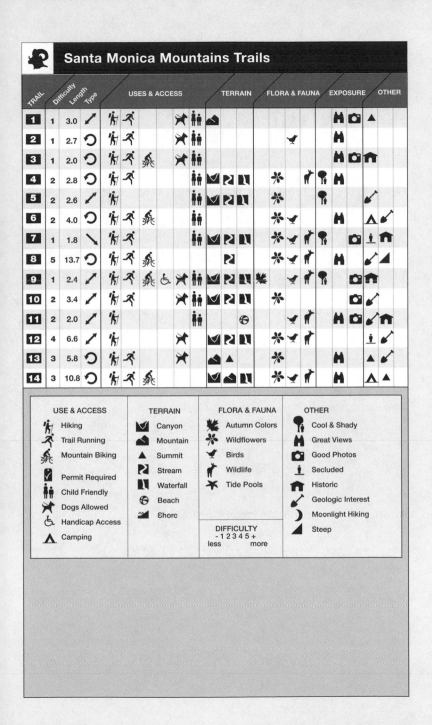

Santa Monica Mountains Trails

TRAIL	Difficulty	Length	Type	USES & ACCESS	TERRAIN	FLORA & FAUNA	EXPOSURE	OTHER
1	1	3.0						
2	1	2.7						
3	1	2.0						
4	2	2.8						
5	2	2.6						
6	2	4.0						
7	1	1.8						
8	5	13.7						
9	1	2.4						
10	2	3.4						
11	2	2.0						
12	4	6.6						
13	3	5.8						
14	3	10.8						

USE & ACCESS
- Hiking
- Trail Running
- Mountain Biking
- Permit Required
- Child Friendly
- Dogs Allowed
- Handicap Access
- Camping

TERRAIN
- Canyon
- Mountain
- Summit
- Stream
- Waterfall
- Beach
- Shore

FLORA & FAUNA
- Autumn Colors
- Wildflowers
- Birds
- Wildlife
- Tide Pools

DIFFICULTY
- 1 2 3 4 5 +
less   more

OTHER
- Cool & Shady
- Great Views
- Good Photos
- Secluded
- Historic
- Geologic Interest
- Moonlight Hiking
- Steep

Santa Monica Mountains

Fern glade *in Cold Creek Canyon Preserve (Trail 7)*

Santa Ynez Canyon 43

Twisted oaks and sycamores and pungent bay laurel trees highlight your trek up the wild Santa Ynez Canyon in Topanga State Park. At the end, after some slip-sliding and rock scrambling, you arrive at an 18-foot cascade.

TRAIL 5

Hike
2.6 miles, Out & Back
Difficulty: 1 **2** 3 4 5

Point Dume 67

Scan the ocean horizon from the edge of the Point Dume escarpment, and explore (at low tide) the biologically rich intertidal zone on the rocky beach below. Luckily, the very lowest daytime tides occur during the best times of the year for sunshine and extended visibility.

Zuma Canyon 71

If boulder-hopping appeals to you as a mode of travel or simply as a gymnastic exercise, then the softly rounded sandstone boulders clogging Zuma Canyon's V-shaped floor invite you to give it a try. The approach is an easy stroll, then the real fun begins.

Sandstone Peak 75

No thorough reconnaissance of the Santa Monica Mountains is complete without a visit to its high point, Sandstone Peak. Luckily, no towering antennas mar the view, which stretches across miles of parkland and a big slice of the ocean.

Mugu Peak 79

Visit a waterfall, ogle spring wildflowers, and climb Mugu Peak, which rises from the sea at the westernmost end of the Santa Monica Mountains.

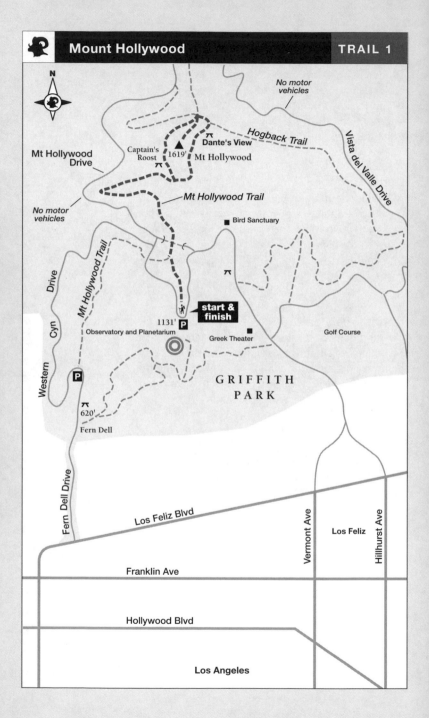

No motor
vehicles

Hogback Trail

Vista del Valle Drive

Mt Hollywood
Drive

Captain's
Roost

Dante's View

1619' Mt Hollywood

No motor
vehicles

Mt Hollywood Trail

Bird Sanctuary

Mt Hollywood Trail

start &
finish

1131'

Observatory and Planetarium

Greek Theater

Golf Course

Drive

Western Cyn

GRIFFITH
PARK

620'

Fern Dell

Fern Dell Drive

Los Feliz Blvd

Vermont Ave

Los Feliz

Hillhurst Ave

Franklin Ave

Hollywood Blvd

Los Angeles

Mount Hollywood

L.A.'s quintessential urban trail takes you to the high point in Griffith Park. On a clear day, your line of sight stretches 50 miles or more, with the city spreading outward toward ocean and mountains.

Best Time

Views are impressive all the way up the trail, and they're truly spectacular when the skies are smog-free. Clear-air episodes occur most frequently between November and March, especially during the early phases of Santa Ana wind conditions, and following the passage of winter storms. Don't take this trail on a smoggy day or you'll be disappointed.

Finding the Trail

From Interstate 5 take Los Feliz Boulevard west to Hillhurst Avenue or Vermont Avenue. Turn right on either street and continue into Griffith Park, following the signs to Griffith Observatory/Planetarium. The main trail to Mount Hollywood begins at the north end of the observatory parking lot.▶1 Posted hours for all Griffith Park roads and trails are sunrise to sunset. Note: if the observatory and parking lot are still closed (renovations will be completed in 2005) you'll find ample parking along the access road.

Trail Description

Follow the trail north (uphill) up along a ridgeline. Dipping just bit, you cross high over a road tunnel; ▶2 listen for horns blaring as cars traverse the tun-

TRAIL USE
Hike, Run
LENGTH
3.0 miles, 2 hours
ELEVATION GAIN/LOSS
500'/500'
DIFFICULTY
– **1** 2 3 4 5 +
TRAIL TYPE
Out & Back
SURFACE TYPE
Dirt

FEATURES
Dogs Allowed
Child Friendly
Mountain
Great Views
Summit
Photo Opportunity

M Great Views

▲ Summit

nel below. Next, a couple of long, lazy switchback legs take you to a trail junction not far below (and south of) Mount Hollywood's summit. On the way up those trail segments, note how Griffith Observatory's domed profile in the south nests in the foreground, while downtown L.A.'s skyscrapers soar behind it. You'll need a telephoto lens to capture that scene effectively. In the west, there's an oblique view of the HOLLYWOOD sign on Mount Lee.

At the trail junction south of the summit,▶3 make a sharp left. Pass shady **Captain's Roost** picnic area (a water fountain is here) and traverse across the west flank of Mount Hollywood. Keep ascending past a large, round water tank. Make a sharp right turn at the next opportunity, and walk up to the picnic tables on the bulldozed summit of Mount Hollywood.▶4 The sole appeal of this barren spot is the tremendous view you get, potentially taking in nearly every major mountain range in the Southland and a good percentage of a populated region of some 15 million people.

On the return, go back downhill about 200 yards, make a sharp right, go past **Dante's View** picnic area ▶5 (drinking water here), and continue your descent—this time along the east flank of Mount Hollywood. You will end up back at the trail junction south of the summit. From there, simply retrace your steps back down the two long switchback segments and return to the observatory parking lot.▶6

🚶 MILESTONES

▶1 0.0 Start at the north end of Griffith Observatory parking lot
▶2 0.2 Pass over tunnel
▶3 1.0 Pass Captain's Roost picnic area
▶4 1.5 Arrive at Mt. Hollywood summit
▶5 1.7 Pass Dante's View picnic area
▶6 3.0 Finish at observatory parking lot

📷 Photo Opportunity

Toyon *(a.k.a. California holly, or Christmas berry) is the "holly"*
of Hollywood. This tree grows abundantly on Griffith Park's hill-
sides. Red berries appear in November or December.

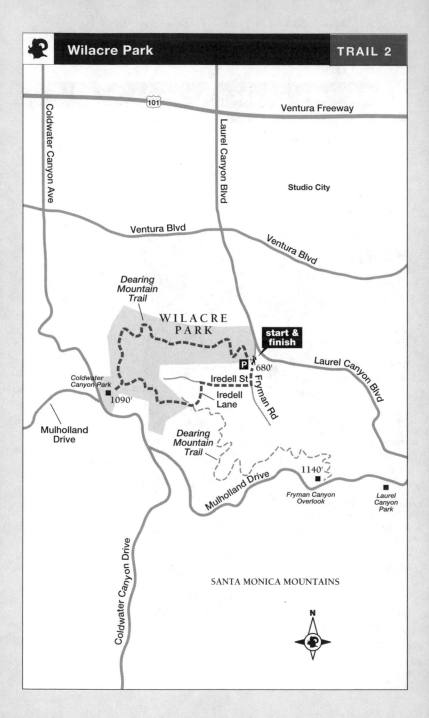

Wilacre Park

TRAIL 2

101

Ventura Freeway

Coldwater Canyon Ave

Laurel Canyon Blvd

Studio City

Ventura Blvd

Ventura Blvd

Dearing Mountain Trail

WILACRE PARK

start & finish

P 680'

Laurel Canyon Blvd

Coldwater Canyon Park

1090'

Iredell St

Iredell Lane

Fryman Rd

Mulholland Drive

Dearing Mountain Trail

Mulholland Drive

1140'

Fryman Canyon Overlook

Laurel Canyon Park

Coldwater Canyon Drive

SANTA MONICA MOUNTAINS

N

Wilacre Park

An island of open space in the midst of Studio City's more lavish residential areas, **Wilacre Park** (the former estate of silent movie star Will Acres) offers a wide-ranging view of San Fernando Valley and a peaceful, quiet atmosphere. This loop route goes up through Wilacre Park and visits **Coldwater Canyon Park**, which is the headquarters of TreePeople, a grassroots organization that is spearheading efforts to plant millions of trees in the urban Los Angeles area.

TRAIL USE
Hike, Run
LENGTH
2.7 miles, 1¹/₂ hours
ELEVATION GAIN/LOSS
400'/400'
DIFFICULTY
– **1** 2 3 4 5 +
TRAIL TYPE
Loop
SURFACE TYPE
Dirt, paved

FEATURES
Dogs Allowed
Child Friendly
Great Views
Birds

Best Time

This trail is fine any time of year since the route is partially shaded and short. But during the warm months it's best to avoid the heat of the day.

Finding the Trail

Exit the 101 Freeway at Laurel Canyon Blvd., and drive 1.4 miles south to Wilacre Park, on the right. Posted hours for the trailhead and trail are sunrise to sunset. If the parking lot is full, find curbside parking nearby, particularly in the direction of Fryman Road, just south. To close the loop you will be walking back along Fryman Road.

Trail Description

From the parking lot,▶1 take the wide, curving **Dearing Mountain Trail** uphill, partly on the remnant blacktop of the driveway into the Will Acres spread. Your ascent is flanked by pine and cypress trees. After passing the slab foundation of Acres' old house, the road turns to dirt. You continue to ascend, more easily now, along north-facing slopes dotted with live oak and walnut trees. After a while you turn south, descend a little, and arrive at a wide junction ▶2 on the edge of Coldwater Canyon Park. Take the Magic Forest Trail on the right, or use some steps a little way to the left to reach the old fire station above that serves as headquarters for TreePeople. Check out the exhibits there, which include a self-guiding tour of TreePeople's nursery.

Return to the wide junction▶3 and continue east (downhill) on the **Dearing Mountain Trail**, After 0.5 mile you hit pavement at Iredell Lane,▶4 a cozy, residential cul-de-sac. The last 0.6 mile is along lightly traveled streets—down **Iredell Lane** to Iredell Street, down **Iredell Street** to Fryman Road, and down **Fryman Road** to the starting point.▶5

🚶	MILESTONES
▶1	0.0 Proceed uphill from the Wilacre Park trailhead
▶2	1.4 Arrive at a wide junction; climb into Coldwater Canyon Park on side path
▶3	1.6 Return to wide junction
▶4	2.1 Reach Iredell Lane; continue downhill on residential streets
▶5	2.7 Finish at Wilacre Park trailhead

California walnut *trees in Wilacre Park are native only to the foothills surrounding the L.A. Basin. In late autumn the yellowing leaves of this tree impart a pale but attractive coloration to the north-facing slopes.*

Fryman Canyon

After following Iredell Lane east a short distance, note the ascending trail on the right. This is the continuation of the **Dearing Mountain Trail**. After two miles of tightly twisting turns and various ups and downs, this segment of the trail reaches the **Fryman Canyon Overlook** on Mulholland Drive.

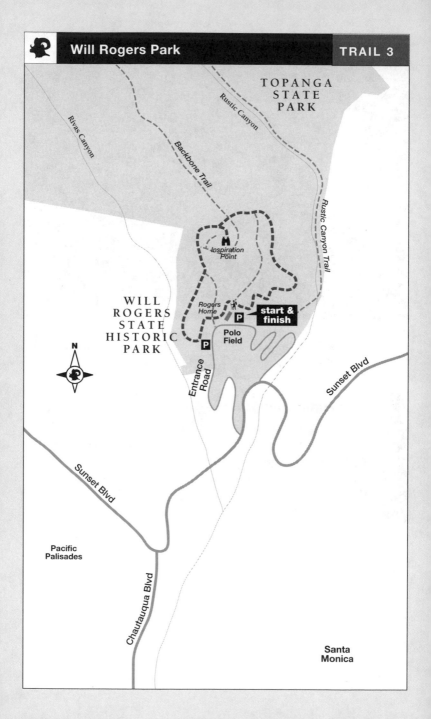

TOPANGA
STATE
PARK

Rustic Canyon

Rivas Canyon

Backbone Trail

Rustic Canyon Trail

Inspiration
Point

WILL
ROGERS
STATE
HISTORIC
PARK

N

Rogers
Home

start &
finish

Polo
Field

Entrance
Road

Sunset Blvd

Sunset Blvd

Pacific
Palisades

Chautauqua Blvd

Santa
Monica

Will Rogers Park

Especially on weekdays or early on weekend mornings, this quiet ramble on the grounds of the historic Will Rogers estate is perfect for getting some exercise. You also take advantage of multimillion-dollar views of Santa Monica, West L.A., downtown L.A., and the blue Pacific Ocean.

Best Time

This trail is best all year, any time of day the park is open, but you will double your pleasure if you experience the view from the top on a crystal-clear day.

Finding the Trail

The entrance to Will Rogers State Historic Park is on the north side of Sunset Blvd., about midway between Chautauqua Blvd and Amalfi Drive in Pacific Palisades. The park is open daily, except certain holidays, from 8 A.M. to sunset. A parking fee is charged. It is possible to park outside (possibly a half mile away) and walk in, however.

Trail Description

The main, wide, 2-mile loop trail begins at the north end of the big lawn adjoining the Rogers mansion.▶1 About half way around the loop, and at its highest point, you come to **Inspiration Point**,▶2 a flat-topped bump on a ridge overlooking the entire Rogers spread. The upscale bedroom community of Pacific Palisades clings tightly to the fluted slopes descending from the Santa Monica Mountains.

TRAIL USE
Hike, Run, Bike
LENGTH
2.0 miles, 1 hour
ELEVATION GAIN/LOSS
350'/350'
DIFFICULTY
– **1** 2 3 4 5 +
TRAIL TYPE
Loop
SURFACE TYPE
Dirt

TRAIL FEATURES:
Dogs Allowed
Child Friendly
Great Views
Photo Opportunity
Historic

Relaxing on the benches at the top on a clear day, you can admire true-as-advertised, inspiring vistas stretching east to the front range of the San Gabriel Mountains and southeast to the Santa Ana Mountains. The flat L.A. cityscape, punctuated by clusters of high-rise buildings, spreads almost as far as the eye can see. South past the swelling Palos Verdes peninsula you can sometimes spot Santa Catalina Island, rising in ethereal majesty from the shining surface of the sea.

Photo Opportunity

Will Rogers

Newspaperman, radio commentator, movie star and pop-philosopher Will Rogers purchased this 182-acre property in 1922 and lived with his family here from 1928 until his death in 1935. He enjoyed strolling about the property. Although historic only by Southern California standards, his 31-room mansion is nevertheless interesting to tour.

Rogers once remarked "...if your time is worth anything, travel by air. If not, you might just as well walk."

MILESTONES

▶1　0.0　Start north of Will Rogers home; stay left on the wide loop trail going behind the mansion and up a slope to the west

▶2　0.9　Arrive at Inspiration Point; return via the east leg of the loop trail

▶3　2.0　Finish at the Rogers home

The polo field in front of the Rogers mansion is used for polo matches on most weekends. You may hear the amplified sound of the properly British-accented announcer for quite a distance up the trail.

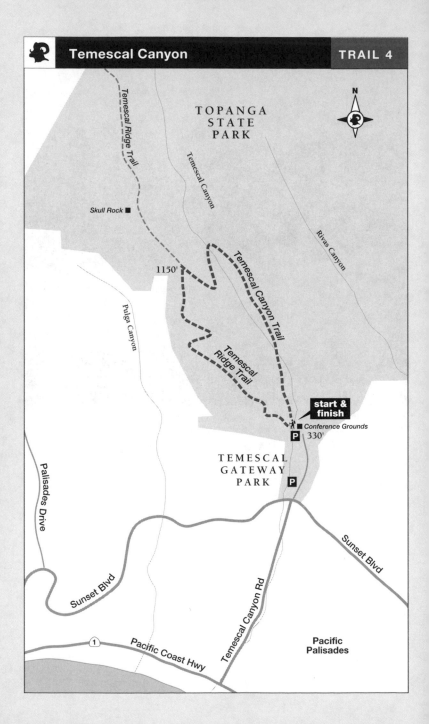

Temescal Ridge Trail

TOPANGA
STATE
PARK

Temescal Canyon

Rivas Canyon

Skull Rock ■

1150'

Temescal Canyon Trail

Pulga Canyon

Temescal
Ridge Trail

start &
finish

■ Conference Grounds

P 330'

TEMESCAL
GATEWAY
PARK

P

Palisades Drive

Sunset Blvd

Sunset Blvd

1 Pacific Coast Hwy

Temescal Canyon Rd

Pacific
Palisades

N

Temescal Canyon

A favorite short trek for exercise minded hikers and runners in the West L.A. area, this loop includes wonderful views from high places, a shady passage through riparian and oak woodland, and seasonal waterfalls.

Best Time

This hike is good all year, but due to the initial climb in full sunlight it's best to avoid the middle of the day during the warmer months of the year.

Finding the Trail

Begin at **Temescal Gateway Park**, just north of the intersection of Sunset Blvd. and Temescal Canyon Road in Pacific Palisades. Park for a fee inside the park, sunrise to sunset, or find a curbside space in the commercial district of Pacific Palisades across Sunset Boulevard.

Trail Description

Using directional signs on the **Temescal Gateway Park** property, head north toward several buildings that comprise the former Presbyterian conference grounds, ▶1 and pick up the **Temescal Ridge Trail**. The narrow trail immediately starts a vigorous ascent up the scrubby canyon wall to the west. After several twists and turns, the trail gains a moderately ascending crest and sticks to it. Pause often so you can turn around and look at the ever-widening view of the coastline curving from Santa Monica Bay to

TRAIL USE
Hike, Run
LENGTH
2.8 miles, 1½ hours
ELEVATION GAIN/LOSS
850'/850'
DIFFICULTY
- 1 **2** 3 4 5 +
TRAIL TYPE
Loop
SURFACE TYPE
Dirt

FEATURES
Child Friendly
Canyon
Streams
Waterfall
Wildflowers
Wildlife
Cool & Shady
Great Views

Malibu. Ahead, two short trails (the Leacock and Bienveneda trails) strike off to the left toward a trailhead at the end of Bienveneda Avenue. Ignore those paths and continue to a junction (1.3 miles from the start) with the former Temescal Ridge fire road,▶2 which is signed **Temescal Ridge Trail** to the north, and **Temescal Canyon Trail** to the south. You'll turn right at that junction and follow the Temescal Canyon Trail into the shady bottom of Temescal Canyon.

At the bottom,▶3 you cross Temescal Canyon's creek on a footbridge. Above and below that bridge are small, trickling waterfalls and shallow, limpid pools. You can poke around the creek a bit for a look at its typical denizens—water striders and newts.

When you've finished sightseeing, continue down the trail back to the conference grounds,▶4 a mile away.

 Dogs

Dogs on leash are allowed in Temescal Gateway Park, but not on the loop route described above, which mostly lies on Topanga State Park land. Hikers and their intrepid pets, however, may greatly enjoy the beautiful new (if somewhat sketchy and poison-oak infested) Rivas Canyon Trail. This 2-mile route ascends east from the conference grounds, tops a ridge, zigzags downward into semi-shaded Rivas Canyon, and finally enters a back corner of Will Rogers State Historic Park.

MILESTONES

▶1   0.0 Follow the Temescal Ridge Trail uphill from the conference buildings

▶2   1.3 Turn right on the Temescal Canyon Trail; descend into Temescal Canyon

▶3   1.7 Cross footbridge over Temescal Creek

▶4   2.8 Finish at conference buildings

OPTIONS

Skull Rock

You can depart from the loop at the north end with a 0.4-mile side trip to Skull Rock, a grotesque sandstone outcrop quite typical of the rock formations in this section of the Santa Monica Mountains.

Live oak, sycamore, willow, and bay trees highlight your final return along the Temescal Canyon Trail, their woodsy scents commingling on the ocean breeze.

Sycamore tree *in Temescal Canyon*

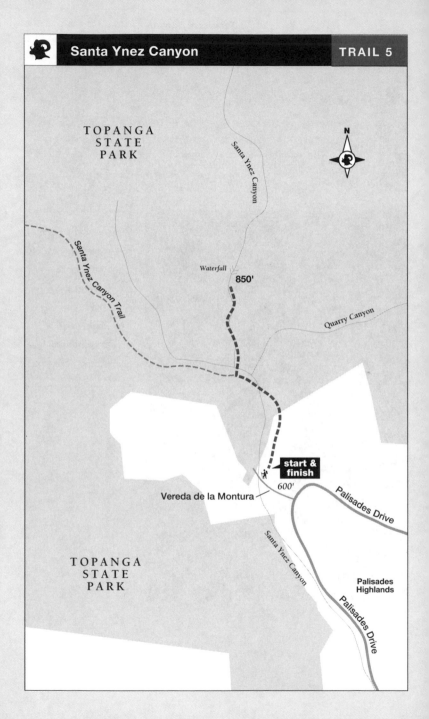

N

TOPANGA
STATE
PARK

Santa Ynez Canyon

Santa Ynez Canyon Trail

Waterfall
850'

Quarry Canyon

start &
finish
600'

Vereda de la Montura

Palisades Drive

Santa Ynez Canyon

TOPANGA
STATE
PARK

Palisades
Highlands

Palisades Drive

Santa Ynez Canyon

Twisted oaks and sycamores and pungent bay laurel trees highlight this brief trek up the L.A. coast's most easily accessible wild, waterfall-bearing canyon. The goal is an 18-foot cascade tucked into one of the several upper branches of Santa Ynez Canyon.

Best Time

Winter through early summer are best to take advantage of the maximum flow of water over the falls. The trail and falls may be inaccessible during and after periods of heavy rainfall.

Finding the Trail

From Pacific Coast Highway in Pacific Palisades, take Sunset Blvd. north 0.5 mile to Palisades Drive, and follow Palisades north for 2.4 miles into the Palisades Highlands housing development and to the street called Vereda de la Montura. Turn left and within a long block find the Santa Ynez Canyon trailhead on the right—a narrow gate unlocked during daylight hours.▶1 There's abundant free curbside parking in the surrounding neighborhood.

Trail Description

After a short descent pick up the trail going up along **Santa Ynez Canyon**. Before long you're dodging stray willow branches, stepping across the soggy creek, and forgetting about the civilized world behind you. After 0.5 mile, the wide mouth of Quarry Canyon, site of an old limestone quarry, opens to the right. Stay left and

TRAIL USE
Hike
LENGTH
2.6 miles, 2 hours
ELEVATION GAIN/LOSS
250'/250'
DIFFICULTY
– 1 **2** 3 4 5 +
TRAIL TYPE
Out & Back
SURFACE TYPE
Dirt

FEATURES
Child Friendly
Canyon
Streams
Waterfalls
Wildflowers
Cool & Shady
Geological interest

go another 100 yards to a second canyon on the right. The main trail going straight leads to the Trippet Ranch headquarters of Topanga State Park. Take the lesser-traveled trail right (north) up the second canyon,►2 which is the major fork of Santa Ynez Canyon.

The California bay, or bay laurel, trees you'll see in Santa Ynez Canyon are commonly found in shady, moist canyons throughout the Los Angeles region. Crush one of the dark, elongated leaves and sniff it to get a whiff of the minty/pungent scent.

Waterfall

After some foot-wetting creek crossings and a slippery scramble over some conglomerate boulders, you arrive at the grotto below the falls.►3 The cascade itself is impressive only after a substantial amount of rain has fallen, but the cool, damp air is always refreshing.

With their orientation subject to deep shadow, the falls in Santa Ynez Canyon are difficult to photograph properly—unless the day is cloudy-bright, in which case the lighting is perfect.

On your return (utilizing the same way back), near the two canyon mouths mentioned earlier, you can look for the stone chimney of a burnt-out cabin and a sandstone boulder pocked by Indian mortars.

MILESTONES

►1 0.0 From Santa Ynez trailhead gate, descend to creek and continue upstream
►2 0.5 Turn right on the narrow trail into upper Santa Ynez Canyon
►3 1.3 Arrive at Santa Ynez Falls
►4 2.6 Finish at Santa Ynez trailhead gate

Eagle Rock's *tilted sandstone strata, pitted with small caves, is an outstanding example of the 15-million-year-old Topanga Canyon Formation that underlies much of Topanga State Park and the adjacent Topanga Canyon (Trail 6).*

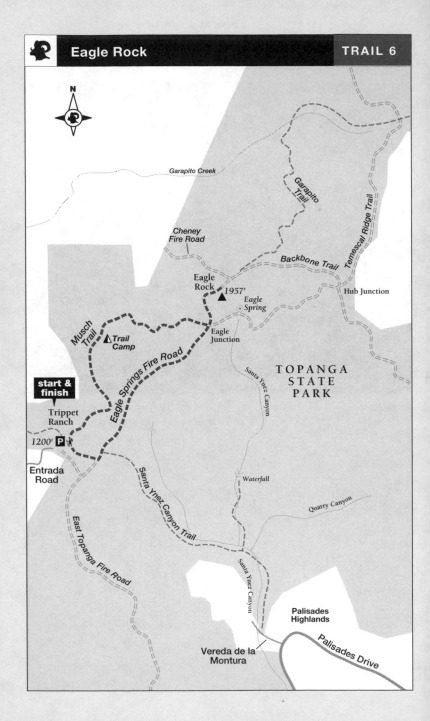

N

Garapito Creek

Garapito Trail

Temescal Ridge Trail

Cheney Fire Road

Backbone Trail

Eagle Rock

1957'

Eagle Spring

Hub Junction

Musch Trail

△ Trail Camp

Eagle Springs Fire Road

Eagle Junction

Santa Ynez Canyon

TOPANGA STATE PARK

start & finish

Trippet Ranch

1200' P

Entrada Road

Santa Ynez Canyon Trail

Waterfall

Quarry Canyon

East Topanga Fire Road

Santa Ynez Canyon

Palisades Highlands

Vereda de la Montura

Palisades Drive

Eagle Rock

Eagle Rock, the most impressive landmark in all of **Topanga State Park**, affords hikers an airy perch overlooking the upper watershed of Santa Ynez Canyon and the ocean beyond. Make it your destination for lunch during a lazy day's hike, or jog there and back in an hour or less.

Best Time

Any time of year is fine, but be aware that most of the route is exposed to sunlight. Cool, dry days are best, when the atmosphere is more likely to be transparent.

Finding the Trail

Take Topanga Canyon Blvd. (Highway 27) south from the San Fernando Valley, or north from Pacific Coast Highway. About midway along the highway's twisty 12-mile course from valley to sea, turn east on Entrada Road (signs for Topanga State Park on the highway alert you to this turnoff). Follow winding Entrada Road, carefully observing directional signs for the park, for 1 mile to **Trippet Ranch**, which is the headquarters for **Topanga State Park**. Pay the state park day-use fee at the entrance station (open 8 A.M.), and park in the large lot beyond.

Trail Description

From the Trippet Ranch parking lot, walk north on a paved drive about 100 yards to where the signed **Musch Trail** ▶1 slants to the right across a grassy

TRAIL USE
Hike, Run, Bike
LENGTH
4.0 miles, 2 hours
ELEVATION GAIN/LOSS
900'/900'
DIFFICULTY
- 1 **2** 3 4 5 +
TRAIL TYPE
Loop
SURFACE TYPE
Dirt

FEATURES
Child Friendly
Wildflowers
Birds
Great Views
Camping
Geologic Interest

Look for hawks, ravens, vultures, and other birds soaring on the sea air moving inland and upward through Santa Ynez Canyon.

hillside. You soon plunge into the shade of oak and bay trees. Enjoy the shade—there's not much more ahead. After contouring around a couple of north-flowing ravines, the trail rises to meet a **trail campground** at the former Musch Ranch.▶2 This camp, along with others to be established along the Backbone Trail, serves equestrians and through-hikers. For now this is the only public camping area in the Santa Monica Mountains east of Malibu Creek State Park.

Beyond the campground, the trail soon starts climbing through sun-baked chaparral. After a crooked ascent you reach a ridgetop fire road at **Eagle Junction,**▶3 from which Eagle Rock, a layered sandstone outcrop, can be seen looming over the headwaters of Santa Ynez Canyon. Turn left and follow the fire road up to the gentler north side of **Eagle Rock.**▶4 Walk to the top for the best view.

After taking in the airy view and a few lungfuls of fresh air, return to Eagle Junction.▶5 This time—for an expeditious return to the start—take the **Eagle Springs Fire Road** running southwest down a sunny ridgecrest. After 1.1 mile, turn right on a narrow trail▶6 going down to Trippet Ranch, or go a little farther down the road to pick up a dirt road that does the same thing.

Topanga State Park offers outstanding opportunities

Eagle Spring

OPTIONS

To extend your hike or run beyond Eagle Rock on the route detailed above, try adding on the fire-road loop to Hub Junction and Eagle Spring (an extra 2.3 miles). Hub Junction is so named for its central location in the state park. A short side path leads to Eagle Spring, where water trickles out of the sandstone bedrock beneath oaks and sycamores.

for **mountain-bike** touring—but not on the exact route detailed here. Bikes are confined to fire roads and prohibited from using single-track trails such as the Musch Trail. The map of Topanga State Park shows some of the ridge-running fire roads by which you can reach Eagle Rock and other points of interest nearby.

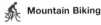

Mountain Biking

🚶 MILESTONES

▶1 0.0 Follow the Musch Trail north from Trippet Ranch parking lot
▶2 1.0 Pass backpacker's trail camp
▶3 2.1 Eagle Junction; turn left on Eagle Springs Fire Road
▶4 2.4 Reach Eagle Rock
▶5 2.7 Arrive back at Eagle Junction; continue south on Eagle Springs Fire Road
▶6 3.8 Turn right on spur trail to Trippet Ranch
▶7 4.0 Finish at Trippet Ranch parking lot

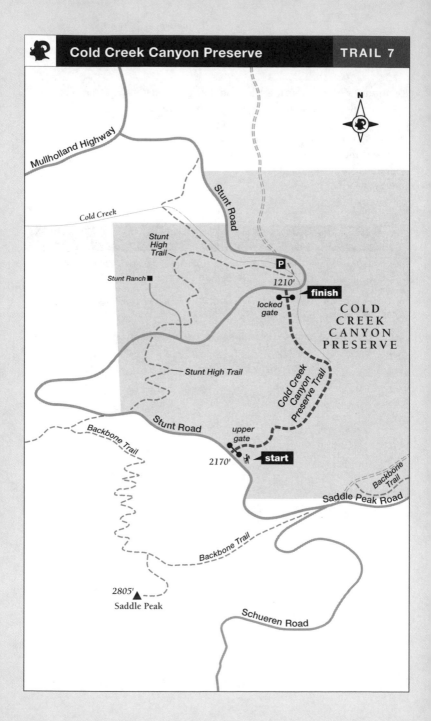

N

Mullholland Highway

Stunt Road

Cold Creek

Stunt High Trail

P

1210'

Stunt Ranch

finish

locked gate

COLD CREEK CANYON PRESERVE

Stunt High Trail

Cold Creek Canyon Preserve Trail

Stunt Road

upper gate

2170'

start

Backbone Trail

Backbone Trail

Saddle Peak Road

Backbone Trail

2805'
Saddle Peak

Schueren Road

Cold Creek Canyon Preserve

Cold Creek Canyon is managed by the nonprofit Mountains Restoration Trust, and is not open to the general public. However, docent-led public hikes are offered here nearly every weekend, and it is possible to obtain a permit from the Mountains Restoration Trust for hiking on your own if you decide to join that organization. The guided hikes are listed and described in the quarterly publication *Outdoors, Santa Monica Mountains Recreation Area*, published by the National Park Service (805) 370-2301. Some of these hikes feature a car shuttle, which allows one-way, downhill travel through the canyon, and that leisurely, informative way of exploring the preserve is described here.

Best Time

Cold Creek runs year-round, and the canyon is pleasantly cool except for perhaps June through September. The canyonside vegetation is most attractive during the green season of March through May.

Finding the Trail

From Topanga Canyon Boulevard in Woodland Hills, follow **Mulholland Highway** 5.5 miles west to **Stunt Road**. Turn left (south) on Stunt Road and drive 1.0 mile to mile-marker 1.0, where there's a large roadside turnout.

This is the usual rendezvous point for guests arriving for the tour. The starting point for the point-to-point downhill hike is the preserve's upper gate some 3 miles higher along Stunt Road.

TRAIL USE
Hike, Run

LENGTH
1.8 miles, 1.5 hours

ELEVATION GAIN/LOSS
1000'/1000'

DIFFICULTY
− **1** 2 3 4 5 +

TRAIL TYPE
Point to Point

SURFACE TYPE
Dirt

FEATURES
Child Friendly
Canyon
Streams
Waterfall
Wildflowers
Birds
Wildlife
Cool & Shady
Photo Opportunity
Secluded
Historic

Trail Description

The extravagant lushness of the riparian vegetation in Cold Creek Canyon is astonishing, especially since the 1993 Malibu fire burned virtually everything here to a crisp.

Starting out on the bed of an old dirt road, ►1 you drop 0.4 mile through tall chaparral to reach the canyon bottom, ►2 which is graced with sturdy live oak and bay trees. The farther and the lower you go from here, the lusher the canyon becomes.

Your guide will point out the remains of an old Dodge pickup truck hastily abandoned at the lower end of the dirt road during a 1973 fire. Thereafter, you continue on a narrower trail threading its way through a fairyland of bracken and woodwardia ferns, tules, cattails, Humboldt lilies, and bright green grass thriving on soggy ground. From here on, you are seldom out of earshot of the canyon's delightful little perennial stream.

You'll stop at the site where a nineteenth-century settler constructed a lean-to between two sandstone outcrops, ►3 The settler raised celery (which still grows wild in the canyon) and hauled his crop down to the stage station at Calabasas.

After nearly 2 miles of travel, you reach the padlocked lower gate ►4 on the lower end of Stunt Road, which securely blocks any access into or out of the preserve for those who don't have a key. The rendezvous point is right across the road.

🚶	MILESTONES	
►1	0.0	Start at upper gate; descend into Cold Creek Canyon
►2	0.4	Reach canyon bottom
►3	1.0	Pass old lean-to shelter
►4	1.8	Finish at locked lower gate

Sandstone Formation *above Corral Canyon Road on Castro Crest (Trail 8)*

OPTIONS

Stunt High Trail

Hikers (or runners) who have the energy and the wherewithal to travel farther can try linking the Cold Canyon trail into a loop route that includes the Stunt High Trail to the west.

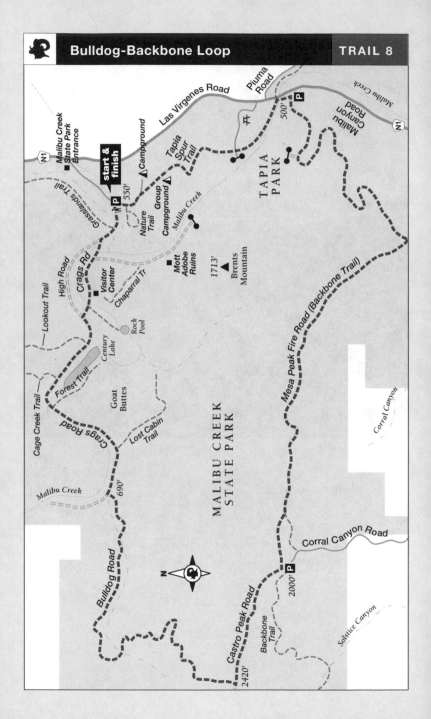

Las Virgenes Road

Piuma Road

Malibu Creek

500'

Malibu Canyon Road

N1

Malibu Creek State Park Entrance

N1

start & finish

550'

△ Campground

Tapia Spur Trail

TAPIA PARK

Grasslands Trail

P

High Road

Crags Rd

Nature Trail

Group Campground △

Malibu Creek

Lookout Trail

Visitor Center

Chaparral Tr

Mott Adobe Ruins

1713'

Brents Mountain

Mesa Peak Fire Road (Backbone Trail)

Rock Pool

Century Lake

Forest Trail

Goat Buttes

Lost Cabin Trail

Cage Creek Trail

Corral Canyon

Crags Road

MALIBU CREEK STATE PARK

Malibu Creek

690'

Corral Canyon Road

Bulldog Road

P

2000'

Castro Peak Road

Backbone Trail

Solstice Canyon

N

2420'

Bulldog-Backbone Loop

This is the classic grand tour of Malibu Creek State Park's rugged backcountry. Along the way you'll tramp or ride along the crestline of the Santa Monicas, circling high above the park's most conspicuous landmarks. Mountain bikers can look forward to a three- or four-hour task. You'd better allow double that amount of time for hiking the route.

TRAIL USE
Hike, Run, Bike
LENGTH
13.7 miles, 7 hours
ELEVATION GAIN/LOSS
2700'/2700'
DIFFICULTY
– 1 2 3 4 **5** +
TRAIL TYPE
Loop
SURFACE TYPE
Dirt

Best Time

Unquestionably, November through April are the most rewarding months due to lower temperatures, no matter what your mode of travel. There's little shade, so be prepared and take along plenty of water.

FEATURES
Streams
Wildflowers
Birds
Wildlife
Great Views
Geologic Interest
Steep

Finding the Trail

From Highway 101 take Las Virgenes Road 3 miles south to Mulholland Highway (traffic light here). Continue on Las Virgenes 0.2 mile farther to the **Malibu Creek State Park** entrance on the right. Pay the state park day-use fee, and drive to the main parking lot, open 8 A.M. until dusk.

Trail Description

From the main parking lot,▶1 head west on unpaved Crags Road. After 0.4 mile you come to a concrete-ford crossing of Malibu Creek. A right at the fork in the road just beyond leads you most directly to the park's visitor center,▶2 open on weekends.

From the visitor center, cross over Malibu Creek on a sturdy bridge and continue up the hill on Crags

Historic

Road, gaining about 200 feet in elevation. Press on past silted-in Century Lake on the left; the Goat Buttes, also on the left; and through the M*A*S*H site, where outdoor scenes for the M*A*S*H television series were recorded. Bird life is abundant along this stretch, where the trail parallels Malibu Creek.

After a total of 2.7 miles, bear left on **Bulldog Road** (Bulldog Motorway),▶4 a fire road that also serves as a powerline access road. The road ascends along a small, oak-shaded creek, then rises crookedly along slopes thickly clothed in chaparral. As you climb, you'll pass side roads leading to electrical transmission towers. The physical effort of negotiating the last, steep, uphill mile on Bulldog Road is rewarded by ever-expanding views over and beyond the now shrunken-looking Goat Buttes. You'll also pass close to some interesting outcrops of sandstone, looking much like gigantic incisor teeth. Turn left when you reach **Castro Peak Road** (Castro Motorway)▶5 at 5.8 miles, and start a descent east. The Malibu shoreline soon comes into view, with a clear-air vista that includes several of the Channel Islands, Palos Verdes, and parts of the L.A. Basin.

As you approach the Corral Canyon Road trailhead parking lot▶6, stay left on the footpath that goes up a hogback ridge bristling with sandstone pinnacles. (Bikers should stay on the roadways instead of taking the footpath.) Going east along this ridge for 0.5 mile, pass an old homesite and several gargantuan sandstone outcrops—worth climbing if you want to take the time. On the east end of the ridge, you drop down to the **Mesa Peak Fire Road**, which doubles as a segment of the Backbone Trail.

At 9.4 miles there's a junction. The road to Mesa Peak goes right;▶7 you bear left, staying on the Mesa Peak Fire Road. You now begin a steady descent along the precipitous west wall of Malibu Canyon. Malibu Creek and the curving canyon highway come into view occasionally, seemingly straight

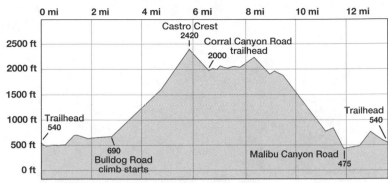

TRAIL 8 Bulldog-Backbone Elevation Profile

down. At 11.2 miles, the fire road abruptly ends at a locked gate just above a water-treatment plant. You sidestep this closure by going right (east) on a more primitive road, again a part of the Backbone Trail. After contouring a while, the trail descends very sharply to Backbone trailhead parking area▶8 along Malibu Canyon Road (11.8 miles). This is a potentially knee-banging drop for runners, and a tricky descent for mountain bikes.

Follow Malibu Canyon Road north, over Malibu Creek, and enter **Tapia Park** on the left, picking up the single-track **Tapia Spur Trail.** That trail skirts some picnic sites, passes the entrance to a private Salvation Army camp, and continues up and over a scruffy ridge to Malibu Creek State Park's group campground. From there, simply walk out the access road and over to your car in the valley ahead.▶9

MILESTONES

▶1 0.0 Follow Crags Road west from main parking lot

▶2 0.8 Arrive at Visitor Center; continue climbing on Crags Road

▶3 2.3 Pass through M*A*S*H site

▶4 2.7 Bulldog Road junction; bear left

▶5 5.8 Castro Peak Road junction; turn left

▶6 6.6 Pass Corral Canyon Road trailhead

▶7 9.4 Mesa Peak junction; stay left

▶8 11.8 Arrive at Backbone trailhead on Malibu Canyon Road; enter Tapia Park just north

▶9 13.7 Finish at Malibu Creek State Park's main parking lot

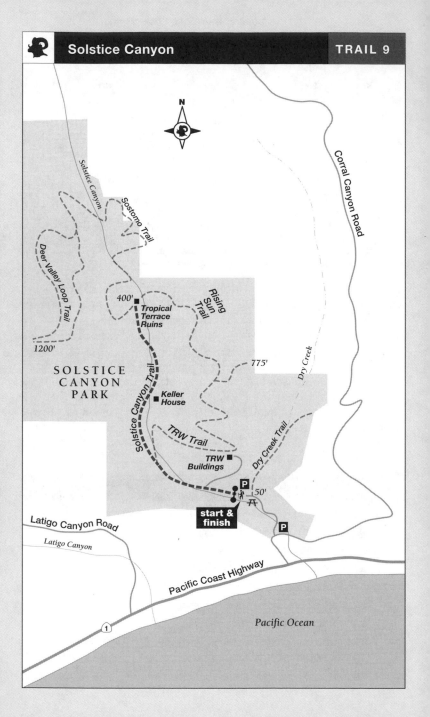

N

Corral Canyon Road

Solstice Canyon

Sostomo Trail

Deer Valley Loop Trail

400'

1200'

Tropical Terrace Ruins

Rising Sun Trail

SOLSTICE CANYON PARK

775'

Solstice Canyon Trail

Dry Creek

Keller House

TRW Trail

Dry Creek Trail

TRW Buildings

P

50'

start & finish

Latigo Canyon Road

Latigo Canyon

P

Pacific Coast Highway

1

Pacific Ocean

Solstice Canyon

The easy-going but superbly scenic Solstice Canyon Trail takes you through the grounds of the former Roberts Ranch—now Solstice Canyon Park, a site administered by the National Park Service. The canyon once hosted a private zoo where giraffes, camels, deer, and exotic birds roamed. At trail's end is Tropical Terrace, the site of an architecturally noted grand home that burned in a 1982 wildfire.

Best Time

All year, any time the park is open, is fine. Strolling here with an umbrella in a light rain is a special treat. Autumn colors are most vivid in November and sometimes into December.

Finding the Trail

The park's gateway is located on Corral Canyon Road, 0.2 mile north of Pacific Coast Highway in Malibu. There's overflow parking space for several cars right at the entrance, and a more spacious lot 0.3 mile farther inside, at the main trailhead. Parking is free but not abundant—carpooling is encouraged. Posted park hours are 8 A.M. to sunset.

Trail Description

Since the **Solstice Canyon Trail** is paved, it accommodates road bikes as well as mountain bikes and all travel by foot. Starting at the main trailhead,▶1 pass through a gate and continue upstream alongside the canyon's melodious creek. You travel

TRAIL USE
Hike, Run, Bike
LENGTH
2.4 miles, 1½ hours
ELEVATION GAIN/LOSS
350'/350'
DIFFICULTY
– **1** 2 3 4 5 +
TRAIL TYPE
Out & Back
SURFACE TYPE
Paved

FEATURES
Dogs Allowed
Child Friendly
Handicap Access
Canyon
Streams
Waterfall
Autumn Colors
Birds
Wildlife
Cool & Shady
Photo Opportunity
Historic

through a fantastic woodland of alder, sycamore, bay, and live oak—the latter with trunks up to 18 feet in circumference. After 15 minutes or so, you pass a stone cottage on the right ►2—built in 1865 by Matthew Keller and thought to be the oldest existing stone building in Malibu.

Historic

At 1.2 miles, you arrive at the remains of **Tropical Terrace.** ►3 Set amidst palms and giant birds-of-paradise, curved flagstone steps sweep toward the roofless remains of what was for 26 years one of Malibu's grand homes. Beyond, crumbling stone steps and pathways lead to what used to be elaborately decorated rock grottoes, and a waterfall on Solstice Canyon's creek. Large chunks of sandstone have cleaved from the canyon walls, adding to the rubble.

Bike riders must return from Tropical Terrace the same way, as they are allowed only on pavement.

MILESTONES

►1 0.0 Start at Solstice Canyon Park trailhead; follow paved path up-canyon

►2 0.8 Pass historic Keller House stone cabin

►3 1.2 Arrive at Tropical Terrace ruins

►4 2.4 Finish at Solstice Canyon Park trailhead

Tropical Terrace *ruins in Solstice Canyon*

Exploring Further

Those on foot may want to try the steep, rugged **Sostomo** or **Rising Sun trails**, which ascend the canyon walls and offer coastline views stretching from the Palos Verdes peninsula to Point Dume. After the arrival of heavy rains, be sure to try the **Dry Creek Trail**, which goes northeast up an oak-shaded ravine for about 0.6 mile before entering private property. An outrageously cantilevered "Darth Vader" house overlooks a sheer precipice in the upper part of the ravine. That precipice becomes a 150-foot-high waterfall after heavy rainfall.

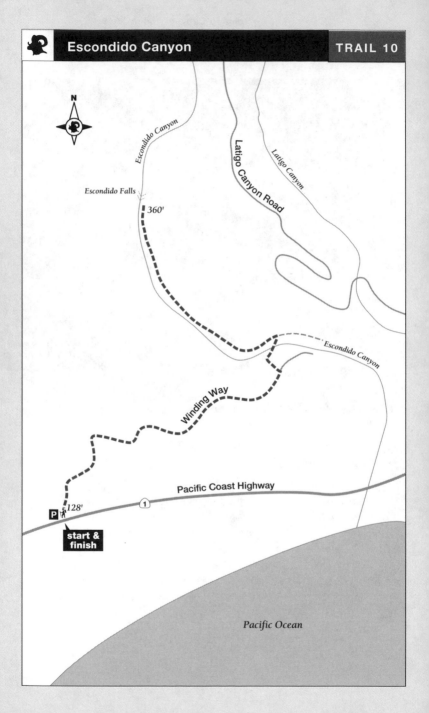

N

Escondido Canyon

Latigo Canyon Road

Latigo Canyon

Escondido Falls

■ *360'*

Winding Way

Escondido Canyon

Pacific Coast Highway

① 1

P ■ *128'*

start & finish

Pacific Ocean

Escondido Canyon

Escondido ("hidden" in Spanish) Canyon conceals one of the natural treasures of the Santa Monica Mountains: a shimmering waterfall leaping more than 200 feet over a broken cliff. Only during times of rare flood do the falls resemble anything thunderous, but even during an average rainy season the intricate dribblings of water are an inspiration.

Best Time

Winter rains, typically arriving in December or January, revive the Escondido Canyon stream. The falls often dry up in late summer and fall.

Finding the Trail

At a point on Pacific Coast Highway 1.7 miles west of Latigo Canyon Road and 1.2 miles east of Kanan Dume Road, turn north on **Winding Way** and look for a trailhead parking lot immediately on the left. Parking is free (daylight hours only). Winding Way itself is a private road, with no parking allowed on its shoulder.

Trail Description

On foot, follow the shoulder of Winding Way (designated by signs as a public access trail), passing palatial new houses perched on rounded hilltops and ocean-facing slopes. After 0.8 mile you come to a summit.►2 Continue 0.1 mile along the roadside, then veer left on a narrow trail descending to the left.►3 After another 0.1 mile you cross Escondido

TRAIL USE
Hike, Run
LENGTH
3.4 miles, 2 hours
ELEVATION GAIN/LOSS
500'/500'
DIFFICULTY
− 1 **2** 3 4 5 +
TRAIL TYPE
Out & Back
SURFACE TYPE
Dirt

FEATURES
Dogs Allowed
Child Friendly
Canyon
Streams
Waterfall
Wildflowers
Photo Opportunity
Geologic Interest

Canyon's stream►4 amid oaks, sycamores, and willows. Turn left when you reach the trail on the far side, heading upstream. Fine displays of sticky monkeyflower adorn the trail in spring and early summer. After the fifth stream crossing, the trail sticks to the east bank and you soon catch a first glimpse of the upper cascades of the multitiered falls dead ahead, its white noise audible over the whisper of the nearby stream.

■ Photo Opportunity

At the trail's end,►5 a faint sulfurous odor in the air is juxtaposed against the sweet sight of feathery ribbons of water draped across a travertine outcrop, which forms the lowest tier of the falls. Don't attempt to climb on or around the falls; just enjoy the soothing ambience of the scene before heading back to the starting point►6 the same way.

A camera with both wide-angle and telephoto capability is useful for photographing the falls. Nearly the entire drop is visible from afar by zooming in. Close to the base of the falls, imaging the lower tier requires a wide field of view.

MILESTONES

►1	0.0	Start at Winding Way trailhead; walk the shoulder of Winding Way
►2	0.8	Pass over a summit
►3	0.9	Take the narrow trail on the left
►4	1.0	Cross Escondido Creek; turn upstream
►5	1.7	Arrive at Escondido Falls
►6	3.4	Finish at Winding Way trailhead

Escondido Falls' *travertine outcrop*

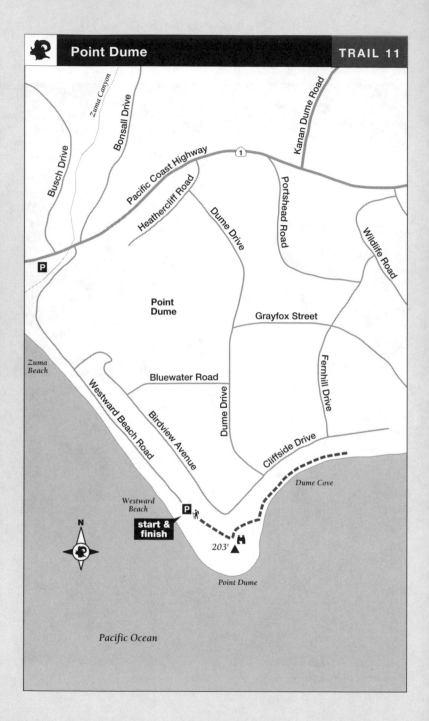

Kanan Dume Road

Bonsall Drive

Zuma Canyon

Busch Drive

Pacific Coast Highway

1

Heathercliff Road

Dume Drive

Portshead Road

Wildlife Road

Point
Dume

Grayfox Street

Fernhill Drive

Zuma
Beach

Bluewater Road

Westward Beach Road

Birdview Avenue

Dume Drive

Cliffside Drive

Dume Cove

Westward
Beach

P

**start &
finish**

203'

Point Dume

N

Pacific Ocean

Point Dume

The southward-pointing promontory of Point Dume, jutting into the Pacific Ocean 19 miles west of Santa Monica, is a widely visible landmark. Just east of the point itself, an unbroken cliff wall shelters a secluded beach from the sights and sounds of the civilized world. The rocky reefs there, underwater most of the time, harbor a mind-boggling array of marine plant and animal life.

Best Time

A pleasant walk anytime the tide is low, this trip is doubly rewarding when the tide dips as low as -2 feet. Strongly negative tides occur during the afternoon two or three times each month from October through March. Consult tide tables to find out exactly when. The lowest tides during the April through September take place during the hours before dawn, so these months are not very good for tide pool-gazing.

Finding the Trail

From the Pacific Coast Highway in western Malibu, turn south toward Zuma Beach and take Westward Beach Road as far as it goes along the coastline. Day-use parking is available there for a fee.

Trail Description

Starting out at **Westward Beach►1** climb the trail slanting left up the cliff. On top you'll come to an area popular for sighting gray whales during their

TRAIL USE
Hike
LENGTH
2.0 miles, 2 hours
ELEVATION GAIN/LOSS
300'/300'
DIFFICULTY
– 1 **2** 3 4 5 +
TRAIL TYPE
Out & Back
SURFACE TYPE
Dirt trail, stairs, then sandy or rocky beach

FEATURES
Child Friendly
Beach
Birds
Wildlife
Tide pools
Great Views
Photo Opportunity
Historic
Geologic Interest

Point Dume *Tilted strata extend into the intertidal zone.*

Sea star *In the tidepools you may find limpets, periwinkles, chitons, tube snails, sandcastle worms, sculpins, mussels, shore and hermit crabs, green and aggregate anemones, three kinds of barnacles, and two kinds of sea stars.*

southward migration in winter. You'll also discover a state historic monument.▶2 Point Dume, you'll learn, was christened by the British naval commander George Vancouver, who sailed by in 1793.

 Historic

As you stand on Point Dume's apex, note the marked contrast between the lighter sedimentary rock exposed on the cliff faces both east and west, and the darker volcanic rock just below. This unusually tough mass of volcanic rock has thus far resisted the onslaught of the ocean swells.

After you descend from the apex, some metal stairs▶3 will take you down to crescent-shaped **Dume Cove**. The going is easy once you're on Dume Cove's ribbon of sand.▶4 The tide pools below the sandy strip (and especially those amid the tumble of boulders right at the tip of Point Dume) harbor some of the best displays of intertidal marine life in Southern California. This visual feast will remain for others to enjoy if you refrain from taking or disturbing the organisms that live there. As a word of warning, be extremely cautious when traveling over slippery rocks, and always be aware of the incoming swells. Don't let a rogue wave catch you by surprise.

Tide pools

As you travel east, the beach widens somewhat. You can walk as far as about 2 miles to Paradise Cove—site of an elegant beachside restaurant and private pier—along a continuous strip of sand, but the first mile of beach travel is the most scenic.

🚶	MILESTONES	
▶1	0.0	Start at Westward Beach; follow trail ascending bluff
▶2	0.2	Visit viewpoint and historic marker
▶3	0.3	Descend metal stairway
▶4	0.3+	Proceed as far as you like along the sandy beach

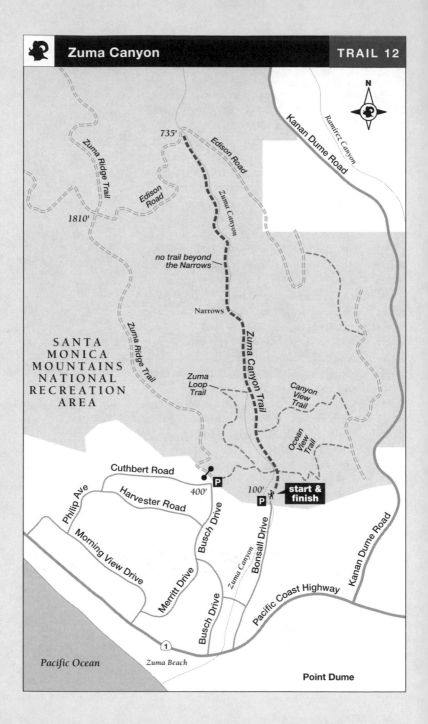

N

Kanan Dume Road

Ramirez Canyon

735'

Edison Road

Zuma Ridge Trail

Edison Road

Zuma Canyon

1810'

no trail beyond
the Narrows

Narrows

SANTA
MONICA
MOUNTAINS
NATIONAL
RECREATION
AREA

Zuma Ridge Trail

Zuma Canyon Trail

Zuma
Loop
Trail

Canyon
View
Trail

Ocean
View
Trail

Cuthbert Road

P

400'

100'

P

start &
finish

Harvester Road

Philip Ave

Busch Drive

Merritt Drive

Morning View Drive

Busch Drive

Zuma Canyon

Bonsall Drive

Kanan Dume Road

Pacific Coast Highway

1

Pacific Ocean

Zuma Beach

Point Dume

Zuma Canyon

Although it slices only 6 miles inland from the Pacific shoreline near Point Dume, Zuma Canyon harbors one of the deepest and most scenic gorges in the Santa Monica Mountains. Under cover of jungle-like growths of willow, sycamore, oak and bay, the canyon's small stream cascades over sculpted sandstone boulders and gathers in limpid pools adorned with ferns. These natural treasures yield their secrets grudgingly, as they should, only to those willing to scramble over boulders, plow through sucking mud and cattails, and thrash through scratchy undergrowth.

Best Time

November through April is best for cooler temperatures inside the canyon. Although the stream may run dry in summer or fall, it's still fun (and actually considerably easier) to rock-hop over the dry sandstone boulders. Possible heavy rains in winter may trigger dangerous flows of water down the upper, narrow section of the canyon, so avoid such times.

Finding the Trail

From Pacific Coast Highway in western Malibu, 1 mile west of the Kanan Dume Road intersection, turn north on Bonsall Drive. Follow Bonsall to its dead end at the mouth of Zuma Canyon. There's free day-use parking here.

TRAIL USE
Hike
LENGTH
6.6 miles, 6 hours
ELEVATION GAIN
700'/700'
DIFFICULTY
– 1 2 3 **4** 5 +
TRAIL TYPE
Out & Back
SURFACE TYPE
Dirt trail, then
boulder hopping

FEATURES
Dogs Allowed
Canyon
Streams
Waterfall
Wildflowers
Birds
Wildlife
Secluded
Geologic Interest

Squirrels, rabbits,
and coyotes are
commonly seen in
Zuma Canyon, deer
and bobcats less so.

 Canyon

Trail Description

Walk past a gate at the end of **Bonsall Drive**►1 and into the sycamore-dotted flood plain ahead. Bypass various side trails branching left and right, and keep straight, crossing the creek several times in the next mile. You'll pass statuesque sycamores, tall laurel sumac bushes, and scattered wildflowers in season.

After about a mile, the canyon walls close in tighter,►2 oaks appear in greater numbers, and you'll notice a small grove of eucalyptus trees across the creek on a little terrace. A short while later, the trail abruptly ends at a pile of sandstone boulders,►3 1.4 miles from the start. Often, water trickles or tumbles past here, disappearing at some point downstream into the porous substrate of the canyon floor. Now you begin a nearly 2-mile stretch of strenuous boulder hopping, up to two or three hours worth depending on the conditions. Some of the larger boulders attain the dimensions of mid-sized trucks, presenting an obstacle course that must be negotiated by moderate hand-and-foot climbing.

Nearby Trails

The narrow side trails in lower Zuma Canyon (Zuma Loop, Canyon View, and Ocean View) are good for tough running as well as hiking—though no bikes are allowed on them. The major mountain-bike route in this part of the Santa Monica Mountains is the **Zuma Ridge Trail**, which ascends a ridgeline west of Zuma Canyon and continues north to Encinal Canyon Road, near Mulholland Highway.

OPTIONS

In upper Zuma Canyon you'll scramble over fine-grained siltstones and sandstones, conglomerates that look like poorly mixed aggregate concrete, and volcanic rocks of the sort that make up Saddle Rock (a local landmark near the head of Zuma Canyon) and the Goat Buttes of Malibu Creek State Park.

 **Geologic Interest**

After a total of 2.8 miles, you'll pass directly under a set of high-voltage transmission lines—so high they're hard to spot. These lines, plus the service road (Edison Road) built to give access to the towers, represent the major incursions of civilization into Zuma Canyon. After another 0.5 mile of rock-hopping, you arrive at the spot where Edison Road►4 crosses the canyon. Turn back and retrace your route, for a total of 6.6 miles round trip.

Alternately—if you want to circle back via the high west wall of Zuma Canyon—climb the Edison Road west to Zuma Ridge Trail, and then follow Zuma Ridge Trail down toward your starting point.

大	MILESTONES
►1	0.0 Enter Zuma Canyon floodplain at the north end of Bonsall Drive; follow main trail along canyon bottom
►2	1.0 Zuma Canyon narrows; continue upstream on trail
►3	1.4 Off-trail travel begins; stay the course upstream over boulders
►4	3.3 Reach Edison access road, a good spot to turn around
►5	6.6 Finish at Bonsall Drive

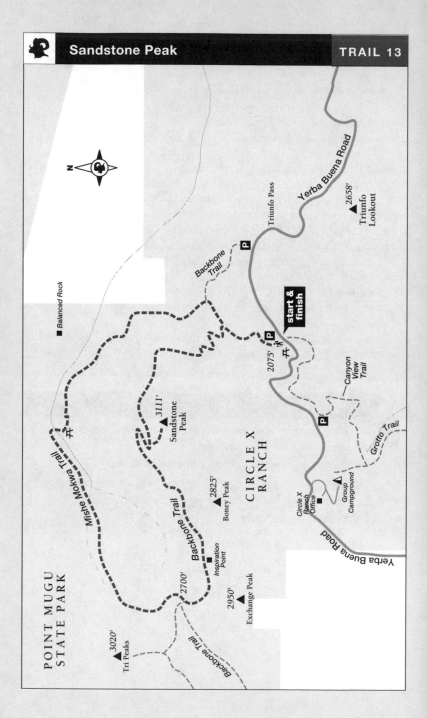

POINT MUGU
STATE PARK

Mishe Mokwa Trail

Balanced Rock

N

Backbone Trail

Triunfo Pass

Yerba Buena Road

2658'
Triunfo
Lookout

start &
finish

2075'

Canyon
View
Trail

Grotto Trail

3111'
Sandstone Peak

CIRCLE X
RANCH

2825'
Boney Peak

Circle X
Ranch
Office

Group
Campground

Backbone Trail

Inspiration Point

2700'

2950'
Exchange Peak

Backbone Trail

3020'
Tri Peaks

Yerba Buena Road

Sandstone Peak

Sandstone Peak is the quintessential destination for peak baggers in the Santa Monica Mountains. At 3111 feet it's the highest in the range, and the one offering the most panoramic view of the coast, mountains, and valleys of the region. You can follow a fire road (Backbone Trail) up to the top and back for a 3-mile round trip; but the far more scenic way to go incorporates the superb Mishe Mokwa Trail into a comprehensive loop of almost 6 miles.

Best Time

Come on a crystalline day in late fall or winter to take best advantage of distant views. Spring is dependably good because of the wildflowers.

Finding the Trail

You'll start hiking at the large trailhead parking lot on the north side of Yerba Buena Road, 1 mile east of the Circle X park office. This same point is 6.4 miles north of Pacific Coast Highway and 4.5 miles west of Mulholland Highway. (Either way you face a white-knuckle drive on the paved, but very narrow and curvy, Yerba Buena Road.) Day-use parking is free at this trailhead.

Trail Description

From the trailhead,►1 proceed past a gate and up the fire road 0.3 mile to where the marked **Mishe Mokwa Trail** branches right.►2 Right away you plunge into chaparral so tall it's often hard to see the

TRAIL USE
Hike, Run
LENGTH
5.8 miles, 3.5 hours
ELEVATION GAIN/LOSS
1400'/1400'
DIFFICULTY
– 1 2 **3** 4 5 +
TRAIL TYPE
Loop
SURFACE TYPE
Dirt

FEATURES
Dogs Allowed
Mountain
Summit
Wildflowers
Great Views
Geologic Interest

Wildflowers

 **Geologic Interest**

outside world. Both your hands and feet may come into play over the next 40 or 50 minutes as you're forced to scramble a bit over rough-textured outcrops of volcanic rock. You'll make intimate acquaintance with mosses and ferns and several of the more attractive chaparral shrubs: toyon, holly-leaf cherry, manzanita, and red shanks (a.k.a. ribbonwood), which is identified by its wispy foliage and perpetually peeling, rust-colored bark. You'll also pass several bay trees, under which the temperature seems to fall about 10°F on a sunny day.

During the springtime bloom along Mishe Mokwa Trail, look for blue-flowering ceanothus, monkey flower, nightshade, Chinese houses, wild peony, wild hyacinth, morning glory, and phacelia. Delicate, orangish Humboldt lilies should be unfolding by June.

After about a half hour on the Mishe Mokwa Trail, keep an eye out for an amazing balanced rock that rests precariously on the opposite wall of the canyon that lies just below you.

By 1.7 miles from the start you will have worked you way around to the north flank of **Sandstone Peak**, where you suddenly come upon a couple of picnic tables▶3 and **Split Rock**, a fractured volcanic boulder with a gap wide enough to walk through.

From the picnic site, the Mishe Mokwa Trail goes briefly north on the bed of an old dirt road. The trail soon turns decidedly west and gradually ascends. You pass beneath some hefty volcanic outcrops and at 2.8 miles come to a junction with the **Backbone Trail.**▶4 That leg of the Backbone Trail, a narrow path, goes west into **Point Mugu State Park**. Keep going straight (south) on the graded fire road ahead, signed Backbone Trail, and gradually circle east.

A few minutes beyond some water tanks on the right, look for a side path going right. ►5 This takes you about 50 yards, to the top of a rock outcrop— **Inspiration Point**. The direction-finder there indicates local features as well as distant points such as Mt. Baldy and Santa Catalina and San Clemente islands.

Press on with your ascent. At a point just past two closely spaced hairpin turns in the wide Backbone Trail, make your way up a slippery path ►6 to the windswept top of Sandstone Peak. On a clear day the view is truly amazing from here, with distant mountain ranges, the hazy L.A. Basin, and the island-dimpled surface of the ocean occupying all 360 degrees of the horizon. In upper Zuma Canyon you'll scramble over fine-grained siltstones and sandstones, conglomerates that look like poorly mixed aggregate concrete, and volcanic rocks of the sort that make up Saddle Rock, a local landmark near the head of Zuma Canyon, and the Goat Buttes of Malibu Creek State Park.

Great Views

To complete the loop, go back down to the road (the Backbone Trail) and resume your travel eastward. One and a half miles of twisting descent will take you back to the trailhead. ►7

🚶	MILESTONES	
►1	0.0	Start at the Mishe Mokwa trailhead; go up fire road
►2	0.3	Veer right on the narrow Mishe Mokwa Trail
►3	1.7	Arrive at picnic area; join wider trail
►4	2.8	West leg of Backbone Trail intersects on the right
►5	3.2	Short side path on right leads to Inspiration Point
►6	4.1	Short, steep side path on right leads to Sandstone Peak summit
►7	5.8	Arrive back at Mishe Mokwa trailhead

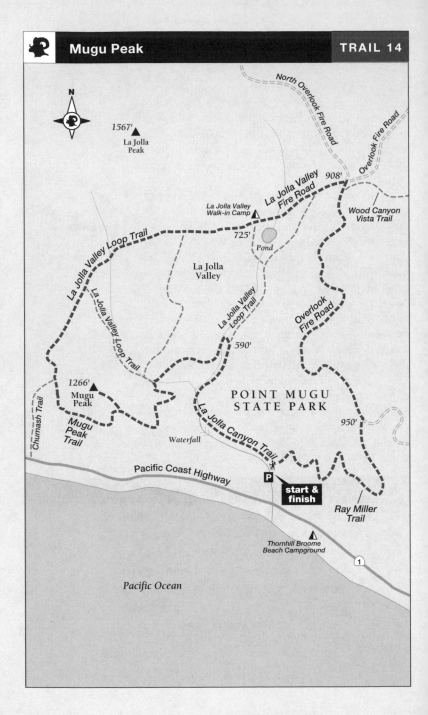

North Overlook Fire Road

Overlook Fire Road

N

1567'
La Jolla
Peak

La Jolla Valley Fire Road

908'

Wood Canyon
Vista Trail

La Jolla Valley
Walk-in Camp

725'

Pond

La Jolla Valley Loop Trail

La Jolla
Valley

La Jolla Valley Loop Trail

Overlook
Fire Road

La Jolla Valley Loop Trail

590'

1266'
Mugu
Peak

POINT MUGU
STATE PARK

Chumash Trail

Mugu
Peak
Trail

Waterfall

La Jolla Canyon Trail

950'

Pacific Coast Highway

P

**start &
finish**

Ray Miller
Trail

Thornhill Broome
Beach Campground

1

Pacific Ocean

La Jolla Valley/Mugu Peak

Mugu (from a Chumash Indian name meaning "beach") lends its name to a rocky promontory jutting into the ocean, to a bald peak towering behind it, and to one of the larger state parks in California—16,000-acre Point Mugu State Park. The big loop we're describing here traverses the unspoiled western quadrant of the park, features plenty of gradual elevation changes, and offers ever-changing scenery.

Best Time

Late fall through winter is best for clear-air ocean and mountain vistas. Spring is best for ogling wildflowers, watching birds, and spotting wildlife. Summer through early fall is normally too hot for a hike or run of this length.

Finding the Trail

Point Mugu State Park lies some 32 miles west of Santa Monica via Pacific Coast Highway. Park at the **Ray Miller Trailhead**, off the coast highway, at the mouth of La Jolla Canyon.

Trail Description

Two trails start from the Ray Miller Trailhead. ▶1 The wide one going up along the dry canyon floor ahead is the La Jolla Canyon Trail—your return route. You will take the narrow **Ray Miller Trail** (which doubles as the westernmost segment of the Backbone Trail) to your right. It doggedly climbs 2.4 miles to a junction with the Overlook Trail, ▶2

TRAIL USE
Hike, Run, Bike
LENGTH
10.8 miles, 6 hours
ELEVATION GAIN/LOSS
1950'/1950'
DIFFICULTY
– 1 2 **3** 4 5 +
TRAIL TYPE
Loop
SURFACE TYPE
Dirt

FEATURES
Canyon
Mountain
Summit
Streams
Waterfall
Wildflowers
Birds
Wildlife
Great Views
Camping

a wide fire road. This is the major ascent along the loop—better to get it over with at the beginning. Ever-widening, spectacular views and good displays of spring wildflowers keep this stretch lively and interesting.

When you reach **Overlook Fire Road**, turn left (north) and wend your way around several bumps on the undulating ridge. At 4.5 miles you arrive at a saddle▶3, where five wide trails diverge. Take the trail to the left (west) that descends into green- or flaxen-colored (depending on the season) La Jolla Valley.

The walk-in trail camp in **La Jolla Valley**▶4 has piped water, restrooms, and oak-shaded picnic tables. From the camp, continue west in the direction of a military radar installation on Laguna Peak. Stay right where marked trails diverge to the left, circling the perimeter of the La Jolla Valley grassland, and rising sharply on the **Chumash Trail**▶5 to a saddle on the northwest shoulder of the Mugu Peak ridge. At that saddle you'll have a great view of the Pacific Ocean.

From the saddle Chumash Trail descends sharply to Pacific Coast Highway. You veer left▶6 on the Mugu Peak Trail, and contour south and east around the south flank of Mugu Peak. You arrive (7.7 miles) at another saddle▶7 just east of Mugu's

TRAIL 14 **La Jolla Valley/Mugu Peak Elevation Profile**

1266-foot summit. Five minutes of climbing on a steep path puts you on top,▶8 where there's a dizzying view of the east-west-oriented coastline, with Pacific Coast Highway sticking close to it.

Return to the saddle east of the peak▶9 and continue descending to a junction▶10 in a wooded recess of La Jolla Canyon. Turn right, proceed east along a hillside, and then hook up with the **La Jolla Canyon Trail**▶11, where you turn right.

 Wildflowers

There's an exciting stretch down through a rock-walled section of La Jolla Canyon, where you'll see magnificent springtime displays of giant coreopsis, which grows mostly on the Channel Islands.

Descending toward the canyon's mouth, you'll pass a little grove of native walnut trees and a small, seasonal waterfall▶12. After a final descent, you arrive at the Ray Miller Trailhead.

MILESTONES

▶1	0.0	From Ray Miller Trailhead, follow Ray Miller Trail uphill
▶2	2.4	Turn left at Overlook Fire Road; follow an undulating ridge
▶3	4.5	Turn left on La Jolla Valley Loop Trail; descend into La Jolla Valley
▶4	5.0	Pass La Jolla Valley walk-in camp
▶5	6.2	Stay right on Chumash Trail; climb toward a saddle
▶6	6.7	Turn left on Mugu Peak Trail
▶7	7.7	Turn left on spur path to Mugu Peak
▶8	7.9	Arrive at Mugu Peak summit
▶9	8.1	Return to Mugu Peak Trail; continue east, downhill
▶10	9.0	Turn right on La Jolla Valley Loop Trail
▶11	9.7	Turn right on La Jolla Canyon Trail
▶12	10.2	Pass La Jolla Canyon waterfall
▶13	10.8	Finish at Ray Miller Trailhead

Giant coreopsis *can stand as much as 10 feet high— head and shoulders above the surrounding scrub. The massed, yellow, daisylike flowers are an unforgettable sight in March and April.*

OPTIONS

Mountain biking is allowed in Point Mugu State Park on paved and graded roads, and on various routes in the Sycamore Canyon corridor, which runs north-south through the central part of the park. The eastern and western portions of the park are managed as wilderness or natural preserve; they are open to travel by foot.

The map shows several ways to **short-cut** the long loop route described above. You can also break up the trip into two half-days by camping overnight at the **La Jolla Valley trail campground**. For more information or to register for that camp, contact the state park office, (818) 880-0350.

La Jolla Canyon

CHAPTER 2

Rim of the Valley

Rim of the Valley

The "Rim of the Valley" wilderness corridor concept envisions a crescent-shaped swath of park land and open space curling around the east and north sides of the San Fernando Valley, reaching into Ventura County to the west. The idea is to keep future development from fragmenting the buffer between L.A.'s metropolitan rim and the Angeles and Los Padres national forests. Spacious public lands along this crescent will hopefully preserve existing wildlife corridors, and also ensure plenty of nearby recreational opportunities for the millions of people living nearby.

The following selection of five trails will introduce you to the best the Rim of the Valley zone offers. On each of the five hikes, a freeway and housing developments lie nearby. Turn away in the other direction, though, and the city completely vanishes.

Permits and Maps

Like the Santa Monica Mountains National Recreation Area (SMMNRA) described in the last chapter, the Rim of the Valley area is administratively Balkanized. **Wildwood Park** is managed by the Conejo Open Space Conservation Agency in Ventura County. **Rocky Peak** and **Rice/East Canyons** are managed by the Santa Monica Mountains Conservancy (SMMC), a state-funded agency charged with acquiring lands from willing private sellers and facilitating public access to those lands. **Placerita Canyon,** which used to be co-managed by Los Angeles County and California state parks, is now under interim management by SMMC. The **Cheeseboro/Palo Comado** park site is part of the SMMNRA, even though it technically lies just outside the Santa Monica Mountains.

Free sketch maps for trails in the Rim of the Valley area are usually available at the trailheads. Among the five destinations described in this chapter, only Placerita Canyon State and County Park charges a fee for entry and parking. No permits are required for the use of the trails in this chapter.

Rim of the Valley

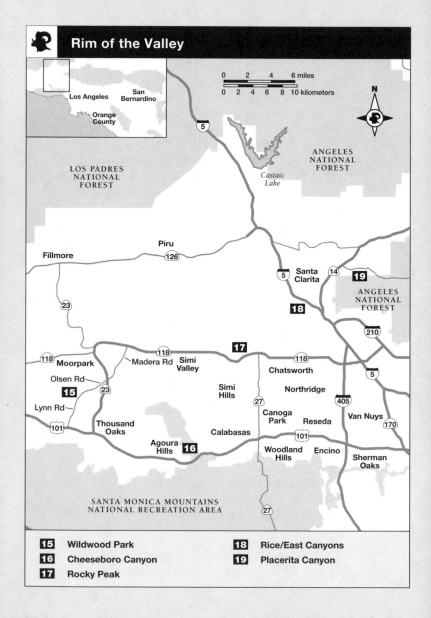

Rim of the Valley

0   2   4   6 miles
0   2   4   6   8   10 kilometers

N

ANGELES
NATIONAL
FOREST

*Castaic
Lake*

LOS PADRES
NATIONAL
FOREST

Piru

Fillmore

126

5 Santa
   Clarita

14

19

ANGELES
NATIONAL
FOREST

18

210

23

118 Moorpark

118

Madera Rd Simi
              Valley

118

Chatsworth

5

17

Olsen Rd

15

23

Simi
Hills

27

Northridge

405

Lynn Rd

101

Thousand
Oaks

Canoga
Park   Reseda

Van Nuys

170

Calabasas

101

Agoura
Hills 16

Woodland
Hills   Encino

Sherman
Oaks

SANTA MONICA MOUNTAINS
NATIONAL RECREATION AREA

27

15	Wildwood Park	18	Rice/East Canyons
16	Cheeseboro Canyon	19	Placerita Canyon
17	Rocky Peak		

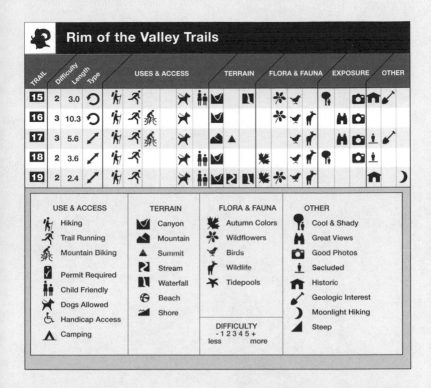

Rim of the Valley Trails

TRAIL	Difficulty	Length	Type
15	2	3.0	loop
16	3	10.3	loop
17	3	5.6	out-and-back
18	2	3.6	out-and-back
19	2	2.4	out-and-back

USE & ACCESS
- Hiking
- Trail Running
- Mountain Biking
- Permit Required
- Child Friendly
- Dogs Allowed
- Handicap Access
- Camping

TERRAIN
- Canyon
- Mountain
- Summit
- Stream
- Waterfall
- Beach
- Shore

FLORA & FAUNA
- Autumn Colors
- Wildflowers
- Birds
- Wildlife
- Tidepools

DIFFICULTY
- 1 2 3 4 5 +
less   more

OTHER
- Cool & Shady
- Great Views
- Good Photos
- Secluded
- Historic
- Geologic Interest
- Moonlight Hiking
- Steep

Bigleaf maple leaves in *Placerita Canyon (Trail 19)*

Rim of the Valley

Live oaks *shade Walker Ranch Campground (Placerita Canyon, Trail 19)*

Placerita Canyon

One of California's historic hot spots, Placerita Canyon hosted California's first gold rush (way back in 1842), and episodes of farming, oil exploration, and movie-making. You can contemplate these historical details as you stroll along the canyon's melodious creek.

TRAIL 19

Hike, Run
2.4 miles, Out & Back
Difficulty: 1 **2** 3 4 5

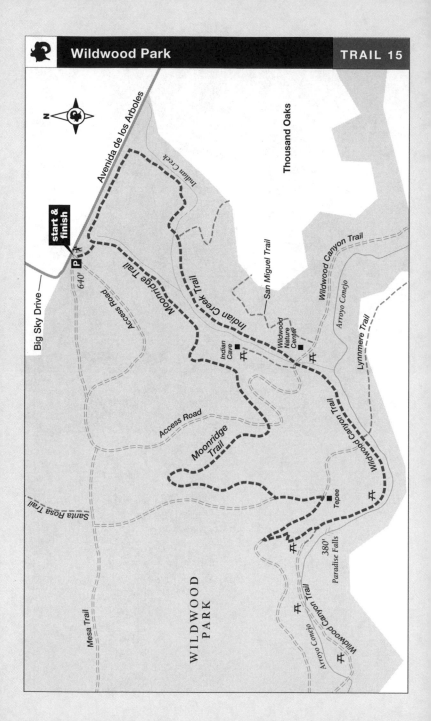

N

Avenida de los Arboles

Indian Creek

Thousand Oaks

start & finish

P

Big Sky Drive

640'

Access Road

Moonridge Trail

Indian Creek Trail

San Miguel Trail

Wildwood Canyon Trail

Arroyo Conejo

Lynnmere Trail

Indian Cave

Wildwood Nature Center

Access Road

Moonridge Trail

Wildwood Canyon Trail

Wildwood

Tepee

380'

Paradise Falls

Santa Rosa Trail

WILDWOOD PARK

Mesa Trail

Arroyo Conejo

Wildwood Canyon Trail

Wildwood Park

If the scenery at Wildwood Park looks familiar, it may be because it's been immortalized in several old Hollywood movies, as well as in television's *The Rifleman*, *Gunsmoke*, and *Wagon Train*. The short but steep hike—down and then up—described here takes you to the park's scenic gem, Paradise Falls.

Best Time

Wildwood Park is most attractive March through June, when spring wildflowers are in peak bloom. The high water table ensures a nearly year-round flow of water in the canyon streams. The trails leading to Paradise Falls are scenic in any season.

Finding the Trail

From Highway 101 in Thousand Oaks, take Lynn Road north 2.5 miles to Avenida de los Arboles. Turn left and follow Avenida de los Arboles 1 mile west. At this point traffic goes sharply right on Big Sky Drive; you make a U-turn and and park on the right at Wildwood Park's principal trailhead, open 8 A.M. to 5 P.M. Nearby curbside parking is also available. Entry into the park is prohibited at night. Adverse conditions may close the park. Park rangers can be reached at (805) 381-2741.

Trail Description

Three trails radiate from the Avenida de los Arboles trailhead. Two are wide and relatively unscenic dirt roads. The third (the one you want), the narrow and

---

TRAIL USE
Hike, Run
LENGTH
3.0 miles, 2 hours
ELEVATION GAIN/LOSS
400'/400'
DIFFICULTY
– 1 **2** 3 4 5 +
TRAIL TYPE
Loop
SURFACE TYPE
Dirt

FEATURES
Dogs Allowed
Child Friendly
Canyon
Streams
Waterfall
Wildflowers
Birds
Cool & Shady
Photo Opportunity
Historic
Geologic Interest

🐦 **Birds**

scenic **Moonridge Trail,**▶1 descends sharply from the east side of the parking area. This is the left side of the parking area as you drive in.

After a short descent, you come to a T-intersection amid oak woods.▶2 Turn right, remaining on the Moonridge Trail. The hand-tooled route ahead descends a sunny slope covered with aromatic sage-scrub vegetation and dappled with succulent live-forever plants sprouting white, comical-looking flower stalks. There's a brief passage across a shady ravine using wooden steps and a plank bridge. At 0.5 mile,▶3 you cross over a dirt road and continue on the narrow Moonridge Trail.

Ahead, the trail curls around a deep ravine without gaining or losing a lot of elevation, edging into the crumbly sedimentary rock. This passage is exciting enough for hikers and potentially terrifying for runners not paying strict attention to every footfall. In fact, there are sheer drops at a couple of spots, so watch those kids! At 0.9 mile you join another dirt road▶4 and use it to descend toward a large wooden "tepee," the so-called **Tepee Outlook** on the knoll just below.▶5 There's a drinking fountain here.

Make a right at the tepee, further descending into the **Arroyo Conejo** gorge. As you descend, watch for the narrow side trail on the left▶6 that will take you straight down to Paradise Falls. The north-facing aspect of the falls makes it difficult to photograph effectively, except on cloudy-bright days or on late afternoons in the spring and summer when the setting sun's rays may illuminate the falling water.

After you've admired the falls,▶7 continue the loop by climbing back up the slope in the direction you came, and by taking the fenced, cliff-hanging trail around the left (east) side of the falls. Beyond the fenced stretch, the narrow trail descends a little and sidles up alongside the creek, where large coast live oaks spread their shade. Soon, you'll find yourself continuing on a path of dirt-road width. Stay with that wide path until you reach a major crossroads,▶8 where the **Wildwood Nature Center** (with a small interpretive display) is around the bend to the right. A short spur path to the walk-through **Indian Cave** lies on the left, and your return route up Indian Creek is straight ahead.

On the **Indian Creek Trail**, you pay your debt to gravity by ascending nearly 300 feet in about 0.8 mile, finally reaching Avenida de los Arboles.▶9 Watch out for poison oak along this stretch. Close the loop by walking on the level alongside Avenida de los Arboles.

The beautifully tangled array of live oak and sycamore limbs along Indian Creek Trail keeps your mind off the climb.

大	MILESTONES	
▶1	0.0	From parking lot, follow the narrow Moonridge Trail downhill
▶2	0.1	At T-junction, turn right, remaining on Moonridge Trail
▶3	0.5	Cross dirt road, remain on Moonridge Trail
▶4	0.9	Turn left on dirt road; descend to tepee
▶5	1.0	At tepee turn right and descend into gorge
▶6	1.2	Take the narrow trail on the left and descend to Paradise Falls
▶7	1.3	From foot of Paradise Falls, climb trail on left (east) side of falls
▶8	1.9	Arrive at crossroads; stay straight on Indian Creek Trail
▶9	2.7	Reach Avenida de los Arboles
▶10	3.0	Arrive back at trailhead parking lot

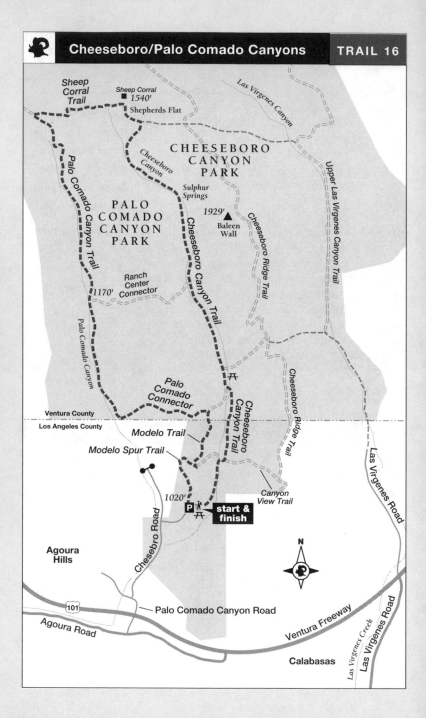

Sheep
Corral
Trail

Sheep Corral
1540'
Shepherds Flat

Las Virgenes Canyon

CHEESEBORO
CANYON
PARK

Cheeseboro
Canyon

Palo Comado Canyon Trail

Sulphur
Springs

PALO
COMADO
CANYON
PARK

1929'
Baleen
Wall

Cheeseboro Ridge Trail

Cheeseboro Canyon Trail

Upper Las Virgenes Canyon Trail

Ranch
Center
Connector

1170'

Palo Comado Canyon

Palo
Comado
Connector

Cheeseboro Ridge Trail

Ventura County
Los Angeles County

Modelo Trail

Modelo Spur Trail

Cheeseboro
Canyon Trail

1020'

P

start &
finish

Canyon
View Trail

Agoura
Hills

N

Chesebro Road

101

Palo Comado Canyon Road

Ventura Freeway

Las Virgenes Road

Las Virgenes Road

Agoura Road

Las Virgenes Creek

Calabasas

Cheeseboro/Palo Comado Canyons

The Cheeseboro/Palo Comado Canyons park site, a unit of the Santa Monica Mountains National Recreation Area, serves as an important wildlife corridor between the interior Transverse Ranges in the north and the Santa Monica Mountains to the south. Self-propelled travelers by the thousands have discovered the site, but there's plenty of room for visitors to spread out. The long, leisurely loop route described here visits the two canyons, both surprisingly serene and pristine despite extensive suburban development in the surrounding region.

Best Time

Without question, the period between the emergence of tender green grass (December or January) and the shift from green to gold (April or May) is the very best time to visit Cheeseboro and Palo Comado canyons. July through September brings midday temperatures in the 90s, making this area unpleasant for all (mountain bikers may enjoy the benefit of evaporative cooling if they move fast enough).

Finding the Trail

From Highway 101 in Agoura Hills, take the Chesebro Road exit, go north about 200 yards on what is signed Palo Comado Canyon Road, then turn right on Chesebro Road. Drive 0.7 mile north to the main entrance to the Cheeseboro/Palo Comado Canyons site, on the right. Gates to the trailhead parking lot swing open at 8 A.M.—but often earlier on weekends, when volunteers staff a National Park

TRAIL USE
Hike, Run, Bike
LENGTH
10.3 miles, 5 hours
ELEVATION GAIN/LOSS
1200'/1200'
DIFFICULTY
– 1 2 **3** 4 5 +
TRAIL TYPE
Loop
SURFACE TYPE
Dirt

FEATURES
Dogs Allowed
Canyon
Wildflowers
Birds
Wildlife
Great Views
Photo Opportunity

Wildlife

Service information booth here. A fenced trail into Cheeseboro Canyon bypasses the parking area, and hikers, bikers, and equestrians use it even when the gates are shut. Be aware that soggy trail conditions may close the park. For more information, call the Santa Monica Mountains National Recreation Area visitor center, (805) 370-2301.

Trail Description

From the trailhead parking lot, follow the wide **Cheeseboro Canyon Trail,**▶1 which goes briefly east and then bends north up along the wide, nearly flat canyon floor. This looks like typical California cattle-grazing land, and indeed it was for a period of about 150 years. Now that the cattle have been removed, oak seedlings are taking root in increasing numbers, and native spring wildflowers are returning to the hillsides, creating splashes of color across the grassy landscape.

At 1.6 miles on Cheeseboro Canyon Trail, near the **Palo Comado Connector** trail joining from the west, you come upon a pleasant trailside picnic area.▶2 Stay on the main, wide trail going north through the canyon bottom. At 3.3 miles you pass **Sulphur Springs.**▶3 As you continue, the oaks

 New Additions

NOTICE

Beginning with the opening of **Cheeseboro Canyon** in the late 1980s, public agencies have been busy buying or trading properties to assemble a huge chunk of open-space centered on Cheesboro Canyon. The newest parcel of open-space land includes upper Las Virgenes Canyon to the east. This addition, along with new public rights of way along fire roads to the north, have opened up opportunities for **mountain-bike** loops of 20 miles or more. The National Park volunteers staffing the information center at the trailhead can give you the latest maps and information.

clustering along the canyon bottom thin out, and you can gaze upward, to your right, at the whitish sedimentary outcrop known as the **Baleen Wall**. By 4.5 miles from the trailhead, in the corner of Shepherds Flat, you'll reach an old **sheep corral ►4** made of wire. Pause here for a picnic, perhaps, before resuming your trip.

From the corral continue west on a narrow trail through the brush. You pass over a saddle and briefly descend to meet the graded-dirt **Palo Comado Canyon Trail** (5.2 miles).**►5** Turn left, and commence a short mile of crooked descent on the wide dirt road. You look down on a tapestry of canyon-bottom woods and slopes adorned with dense patches of chaparral and sandstone outcrops. Soon you are amid those woods,**►6** which are mostly live oaks and sycamores. The going is easy for another two miles as you proceed downhill along the canyon bottom.

At 8.2 miles, there's a forced left turn out of the canyon (off-limits private land lies ahead) and onto the Palo Comado Connector trail.**►7** You meander uphill for a mile to a rounded ridge, where you meet the **Modelo Trail** on the right.**►8** Use it, and later the Modelo Spur Trail, to return to the trailhead by the most expeditious route.

> Let your nose be your guide for locating Sulphur Springs. There's not much to see—the springs are mere seeps.

🚶	MILESTONES	
►1	0.0	Follow the Cheeseboro Canyon Trail
►2	1.6	Picnic area; stay on main trail
►3	3.3	Pass Sulphur Springs
►4	4.5	Visit old corral in Shepherds Flat; continue west
►5	5.2	Turn left on Palo Comado Canyon Trail
►6	6.2	Enter woods
►7	8.2	Turn left on Palo Comado Connector trail
►8	9.2	Turn right on Modelo Trail; continue on Modelo Spur Trail
►9	10.3	Arrive back at trailhead

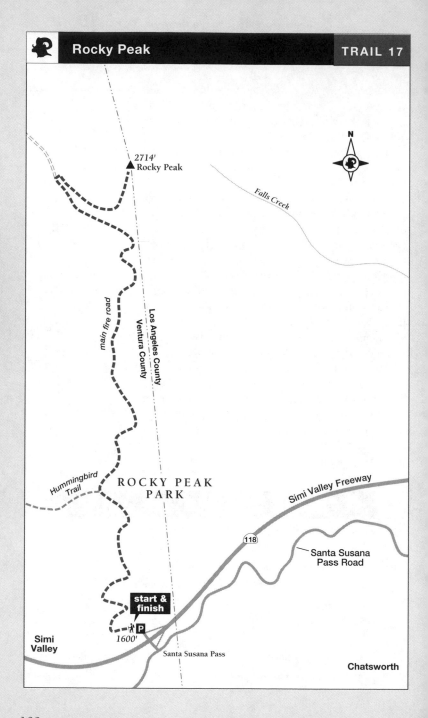

2714'
Rocky Peak

Falls Creek

N

main fire road

Los Angeles County
Ventura County

Hummingbird
Trail

ROCKY PEAK
PARK

Simi Valley Freeway

118

Santa Susana
Pass Road

start &
finish

1600'

Simi
Valley

Santa Susana Pass

Chatsworth

Rocky Peak

Long locked up in private ownership, **Rocky Peak Park** now welcomes hikers and mountain bikers, who can start their trip, conveniently enough, right at the end of a freeway offramp. Nearly the entire approach is lined with dramatic outcrops of beige sandstone. Hikers and runners can proceed uphill all the way to Rocky Peak's summit. Mountain bikers will have to dismount short of the summit, and engage in some boulder hopping to reach the top.

Best Time

Giant boulder piles are fascinating at any time, but only on crystal-clear days is the panoramic view from the Rocky Peak ridge truly rewarding. Early morning, November through March, usually works best. Rocky Peak stands right above Chatsworth, which is the warmest corner of the San Fernando Valley; avoid a summer visit unless you start at dawn.

Finding the Trail

From the San Fernando Valley, take the 118 Freeway west and exit at the Santa Susana Pass/Rocky Peak offramp. Park in the dirt lot on the right. Those approaching eastbound on 118 from Simi Valley and Ventura County will find there is no eastbound offramp at the pass. Instead, exit 118 at Kuehner Drive and go south on Kuehner. Kuehner bends east and becomes Santa Susana Pass Road. Continue to the top of the pass and cross north over the freeway to the trailhead parking area. The park's posted hours are sunrise to sunset.

TRAIL USE
Hike, Run, Bike
LENGTH
5.6 miles, 3 hours
ELEVATION GAIN/LOSS
1200'/1200'
DIFFICULTY
– 1 2 **3** 4 5 +
TRAIL TYPE
Out & Back
SURFACE TYPE
Dirt

FEATURES
Dogs Allowed
Mountain
Summit
Birds
Wildlife
Geologic Interest
Great Views
Photo Opportunity

Rocky Peak's *impressively huge and intricate rock piles are the result of weathering and erosion upon a big block of 65-million-year old sandstone, "recently" (geologically speaking) elevated to its present lofty position.*

Raptors nest on the more remote sandstone outcroppings and overhangs.

Trail Description

Ascent begins immediately on the dirt fire road slanting uphill from the parking lot. ▶1 At 0.8 mile, note that the Hummingbird Trail on the left departs from the road. It goes west over a small rise and then sharply downhill to a trailhead at the north end of Kuehner Drive in **Simi Valley**. Keep climbing on the main fire road. At about 1.5 miles, your relentless ascent is temporarily reversed by a brief drop ▶2 into a little flat where, on the right, you can find shade and rest under a lone live oak tree.

After passing larger and more impressively con-
voluted outcrops of sandstone, the fire road tops out
on a prominent ridgeline (2.4 miles). There, an
older, disused road joins on the right, ▶3 leading cir-
cuitously toward **Rocky Peak**—only a little higher
but well worth a side trip of 0.4 mile for the sake of
a fabulous view. This old road peters out quickly, but
hikers (and mountain bikers, if only for a short way)
can follow an informal path ahead. As the path
becomes indistinct, you face a somewhat scratchy
scramble over a false summit, down, and back up to
the highest pile of boulders. ▶4

Before becoming public land in 1998, Rocky
Peak Park's 4815 acres were partially owned by
entertainers Bob and Delores Hope. The boulder-
studded landscape of this and other properties in
the area have served as a backdrop for many an old
Western film.

 Historic

The Rocky Peak summit defines a waypoint on
the boundary between Los Angeles County and
Ventura County. The view from the top at best
encompasses large parts of these two counties, plus
the Pacific Ocean—partly obscured by the undulating Santa Monica Mountains.

🚶	MILESTONES
▶1	0.0 Ascend on the fire road
▶2	1.5 Ascent is relieved by a brief drop
▶3	2.4 Fire road tops ridge; turn right on side road and continue toward highest elevation ahead
▶4	2.8 Rocky Peak summit; return by the same route

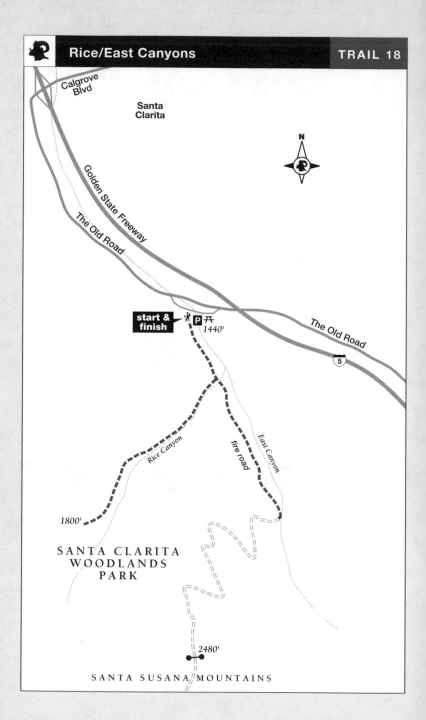

Calgrove
Blvd

Santa
Clarita

N

Golden State Freeway

The Old Road

start &
finish
P
1440'

The Old Road

5

Rice Canyon

fire road

East Canyon

1800'

SANTA CLARITA
WOODLANDS
PARK

2480'

SANTA SUSANA MOUNTAINS

Rice/East Canyons

Rice Canyon and East Canyon drain the steep, north-facing slopes of the Santa Clarita Woodlands not far from the crest of the Santa Susana Mountains. The area receives an average of 20 inches of rainfall annually—just enough, in an environment sheltered from sun's south-slanting rays, to support small canyon streams and an island-like array of scraggly bigcone Douglas-fir trees perched on the hillsides. The route described here visits the bottoms of both canyons.

Best Time

Winter through spring is best for an abundance of water. Late summer through early fall is a bit too hot and dry, though quite tolerable if you get an early start.

Finding the Trail

North of the San Fernando Valley, Interstate 5 rises to a summit and then descends into the Santa Clarita Valley. Near the bottom of that hill, take the Calgrove Blvd. exit. Cross under the freeway to the west side and follow the frontage road, signed **The Old Road**, 0.8 mile south, to the Rice/East Canyons trailhead on the right. This is just before The Old Road goes under Interstate 5. Posted hours at the trailhead are sunrise to sunset.

Trail Description

You'll start►1 with an uninteresting stroll down a fire road (once called the Saugus to the Sea Road)

TRAIL USE
Hike, Run
LENGTH
3.6 miles, 2 hours
(both canyons)
ELEVATION GAIN/LOSS
500'/500'
DIFFICULTY
– 1 **2** 3 4 5 +
TRAIL TYPE
Out & Back
SURFACE TYPE
Dirt

FEATURES
Dogs Allowed
Child Friendly
Canyon
Autumn Colors
Birds
Wildlife
Cool & Shady
Photo Opportunity
Secluded

In the late autumn, the yellowing sycamore and cottonwood trees along both canyons contrast with the dark and somber aspect of the shadowing oaks.

 Autumn Colors

heading into **East Canyon**. At 0.3 mile, you may spot an old water trough on the left and other evidence of past cattle ranching. On the right at this point, ▶2 find and follow a narrow trail. No mountain bikes are allowed in Rice Canyon, and the rough trail is tough on runners, but the scenery on the 1-mile path ahead is enchanting for kids and adults alike. It's a veritable fairyland, complete with a limpid brook and a shade-giving assortment of sycamore, willow, and cottonwood trees, plus four kinds of oak: scrub oak, coast live oak, canyon live oak, and valley oak.

In the upper part of **Rice Canyon**, the trail begins to rise sharply along the slope to the right. After climbing for a few minutes, you get a nice view of steep slopes all around, and glimpses of bigcone Douglas-firs higher up and across the canyon.

Retrace your steps back to the fire road, and turn right when you get there. ▶3 You're now going

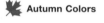

OPTIONS

Canyon Loop

Farther north on The Old Road, closer to Calgrove Boulevard, you probably noticed the signs for **Ed Davis Park** and **Towsley Canyon**. The Towsley Canyon/Wiley Canyon loop through this area of the Santa Clarita Woodlands is nearly as rewarding as East and Rice canyons, though the vegetation is somewhat drier.

gradually uphill along the bottom of East Canyon, which is agreeably adorned with massive, shade-giving oaks. Easy walking ends after about 0.5 mile, exactly where the fire road pitches seriously upward on the right,►4 beginning a curvy ascent toward the summit ridge of the **Santa Susana Mountains**. This is the place for casual hikers to turn around and return to the trailhead.►5

East Canyon

Exercise-minded hikers, mountain bikers, and runners alike can follow the East Canyon fire road from the trailhead to a point 2.2 miles up the mountainside. At that point a gate blocks further unauthorized travel—but by then you've passed a number of bigcone Douglas-firs close at hand and many more are visible on the slopes to the west.

 Canyon

🚶	MILESTONES
►1	0.0 From trailhead, follow fire road into East Canyon
►2	0.3 Rice Canyon hiking trail on the right; follow this side path one mile out and back
►3	2.3 Return to East Canyon, turn right on fire road
►4	2.8 Fire road veers right and starts steep ascent ahead; turn around
►5	3.6 Arrive back at trailhead

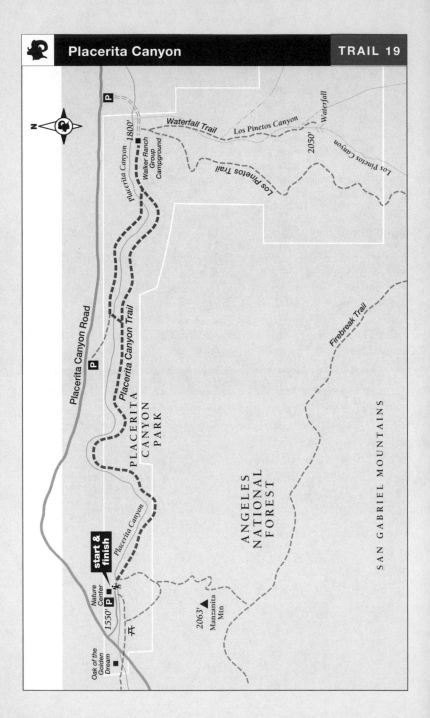

N

Placerita Canyon Road

P

P

Waterfall Trail   Los Pinetos Canyon   Waterfall

Walker Ranch Group Campground

Placerita Canyon

1800'

2050'

Los Pinetos Canyon

Los Pinetos Trail

Placerita Canyon Trail

Firebreak Trail

PLACERITA CANYON PARK

ANGELES NATIONAL FOREST

SAN GABRIEL MOUNTAINS

Placerita Canyon

start & finish

Nature Center

1550'

P

2063' Manzanita Mtn

Oak of the Golden Dream

Placerita Canyon

The highlight of Placerita Canyon's fascinating history was the discovery of gold here in 1842. That event, which touched off California's first gold rush (a rather trivial one at that), predated by six years John Marshall's discovery of gold at Sutter's Mill in Northern California. In the early 1900s, Placerita settlers grew vegetables and fruit, raised animals, and tapped some small reserves of a very high-grade "white" oil. By mid-century, Placerita Canyon had become yet another generic site location for television and movie productions. Both human history and plenty of natural history are in abundance as you stroll the easy-going streamside trail along the most picturesque section of the canyon.

Best Time

Any time of year is good, though the 9 A.M. opening of the gates makes it difficult to take advantage of the early morning coolness during the summertime. The canyon's melodious creek flows decently in winter and spring. During the fall, when the creek is bone dry, you can make your own music by crunching through the crispy leaf litter of the sycamores.

Finding the Trail

Take the Placerita Canyon exit from Antelope Valley Freeway (Highway 14) at Newhall, and drive east 1.5 miles on Placerita Canyon Road to reach the park's main gate, open 9 A.M. to 5 P.M. Drive inside and head for the **nature center** parking lot. Placerita Canyon Park's phone number is (661) 259-7721.

TRAIL USE
Hike, Run

LENGTH
2.4 miles, 1.5 hours

ELEVATION GAIN/LOSS
350'/350'

DIFFICULTY
− 1 **2** 3 4 5 +

TRAIL TYPE
Out & Back

SURFACE TYPE
Dirt

FEATURES
Dogs Allowed
Child Friendly
Canyon
Streams
Waterfall
Autumn Colors
Wildflowers
Birds
Wildlife
Photo Opportunity
Historic
Moonlight Hiking

Trail Description

Starting at the nature center,►1 cross a bridge and pick up the trail heading east up the canyon's live-oak-shaded flood plain. Down by the grassy banks you'll see wild blackberry vines, lots of willows, and occasionally sycamore, cottonwood and alder trees.

After a while, the canyon narrows and becomes a rocky gorge. Soaring walls tell the story of thousands of years of natural erosion, as well as the destructive effects of hydraulic mining, which involved aiming high-pressure water hoses at hillsides to loosen and wash away ores. Used extensively in Northern California during the latter Gold Rush, "hydraulicking" was finally banned in 1884 after catastrophic damages to waterways and farms downstream.

 Historic

Several hundred thousand dollars worth of gold (tens of millions in modern value) were ultimately recovered from Placerita, but at considerable cost, both monetarily and environmentally.

At about 1 mile you reach a split.►2 The right fork climbs a little onto the chaparral-clad slopes to the south, while the left branch connects with a trail going up to a parking area on Placerita Canyon Road and then goes upstream, along the willow-choked canyon bottom. Follow either branch but take the other during your return leg of the hike.

OPTIONS

Los Pinetos

From Walker Ranch campground, the **Los Pinetos Trail** runs south (uphill) toward the crest of the San Gabriel Mountain. A spur path, diverging from that trail at a point near the campground, leads to a small waterfall in **Los Pinetos Canyon**. Either or both of these trails may be followed if you want to increase your mileage while visiting the park.

Using either route, you eventually reach the scant remains of some early-20th-Century cottages hand-built by settler Frank Walker, his wife, and some of his 12 children. The area is now the site of the park's group campground▶3 (drinking water is available here). Amid a parklike setting of live oaks and gentle slopes, you'll discover a sturdy chimney and a cement foundation. Back by the nature center stands another cabin built by Walker, but modified later for use in the television series *Hopalong Cassidy*.

After visiting the serene campground setting, and perhaps having a trailside snack, turn around and start your return.

Nature Center

Placerita's superb nature center houses exhibits on the history, pre-history, geology, plants, and wildlife of the area. Adjoining the nature center are three short, kid-friendly, self-guiding nature trails. Don't miss the wheelchair-accessible Heritage Trail, which crosses under Placerita Canyon Road and leads to the "Oak of the Golden Dream," the exact site (according to legend, anyway) where gold was discovered in 1842 by a herdsman pulling up wild onions for his after-siesta meal.

🚶	MILESTONES
▶1	0.0 From nature center, follow trail into Placerita Canyon
▶2	1.0 Trail splits; go either way, as both join later
▶3	1.8 Walker Ranch group campground; turn around and head back

San Gabriel Mountains

San Gabriel Mountains

Rising to a maximum elevation of 10,000 feet, the San Gabriel Mountains cover a patch of territory stretching 60 miles long (measured east-west), and up to 25 miles wide (north-south). Unlike the Santa Monica Mountains, civilization has made comparatively smaller inroads into the San Gabriels—though this has not been for lack of trying. With periodic fires, floods, and landslides, the mountains beckon visitors to explore and enjoy, but not necessarily to stay and put down roots.

The abrupt ascent of the San Gabriel Mountains from the floor of L.A. Basin is astonishing. Even more amazing is the sharpness of the boundary between city and wilderness—the so-called urban-wildland interface. House pets living on the city side of the boundary routinely get snatched up in the jaws of patrolling coyotes, while black bears have been known to cross the line to enjoy a cooling dip in suburban backyard pools.

For wilderness explorers this abrupt boundary means one thing: you don't have to drive very far to reach lots of rugged, beautiful country. Several of the trails in this chapter originate right on or very near the urban-wildland interface, and many others involve a drive up into the San Gabriels via the view-rich Angeles Crest Highway. Sometimes half the fun of exploring these mountains is seeing the sights along the way to the trailhead.

Permits and Maps

Nearly all the recreational resources of the San Gabriel Mountains are under the jurisdiction of Angeles National Forest. Nearly all of the trails described in this chapter originate on forest-service land.

The immediate consequence for you as a recreating visitor is that, with few exceptions, you must display a "National Forest Adventure Pass"—basically a parking permit—on your car. Ticket-writing staff aggressively patrol the roadsides and picnic grounds of the San Gabriel Mountains, especially on weekends, looking for violators.

The adventure passes sold in Southern California are valid for all four national forests in the state's southern region: the Angeles, San Bernardino,

Cleveland, and Los Padres national forests. The passes are sold at forest-service offices, visitor centers and ranger stations, and through hundreds of independent vendors (mostly outdoor-related businesses). The cost is $5 for a one-day pass, and $30 for an annual pass. Choosing the yearly option gives you a lot more opportunity to make spontaneous trips into the mountains without having to worry about collecting a citation on the windshield of your parked car.

Wilderness permits for day or overnight use must be obtained for two trails described in this chapter: East Fork San Gabriel River and Cucamonga Peak. No other permits, aside from the Adventure Pass, are required for the other trails.

The comprehensive Angeles National Forest recreation map, showing roads and trails, and property boundaries between public and private lands in the San Gabriels, is available for sale at forest-service offices, visitor centers, and ranger stations. Tom Harrison Cartography publishes topographic maps of the San Gabriel Mountains as a whole, plus detail maps of the "Front Range" and "High Country" areas. Free sketch maps of the trail systems in selected areas of the San Gabriel Mountains are also available from the Forest Service, but these are of limited use. For driving purposes, the Automobile Club of Southern California's "Los Angeles and Orange Counties and Vicinity" map can't be beat.

The Angeles National Forest Supervisor's Office, along with a visitor information center, is located at 701 North Santa Anita Avenue in Arcadia. Phone is (626) 574-5200.

Sighting tubes *at Mount Lowe's Inspiration Point indicate distant landmarks (Trail 24)*

San Gabriel Mountains

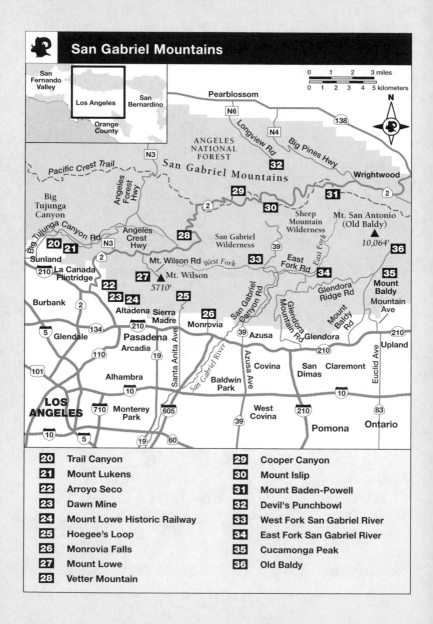

20	Trail Canyon	**29**	Cooper Canyon
21	Mount Lukens	**30**	Mount Islip
22	Arroyo Seco	**31**	Mount Baden-Powell
23	Dawn Mine	**32**	Devil's Punchbowl
24	Mount Lowe Historic Railway	**33**	West Fork San Gabriel River
25	Hoegee's Loop	**34**	East Fork San Gabriel River
26	Monrovia Falls	**35**	Cucamonga Peak
27	Mount Lowe	**36**	Old Baldy
28	Vetter Mountain		

San Gabriel Mountains Trails

TRAIL	Difficulty	Length	Type	USES & ACCESS	TERRAIN	FLORA & FAUNA	EXPOSURE	OTHER
20	2	3.0						
21	4	8.4						
22	3	10.0						
23	3	5.6						
24	4	11.4						
25	2	5.3						
26	1	1.6						
27	2	3.2						
28	1	1.4						
29	2	3.0						
30	2	5.6						
31	3	7.6						
32	3	6.2						
33	3	12.6						
34	3	9.6						
35	4	12.0						
36	3	6.4						

USE & ACCESS
- Hiking
- Trail Running
- Mountain Biking
- Permit Required
- Child Friendly
- Dogs Allowed
- Handicap Access
- Camping

TERRAIN
- Canyon
- Mountain
- Summit
- Stream
- Waterfall
- Beach
- Shore

FLORA & FAUNA
- Autumn Colors
- Wildflowers
- Birds
- Wildlife
- Tidepools

OTHER
- Cool & Shady
- Great Views
- Good Photos
- Secluded
- Historic
- Geologic Interest
- Moonlight Hiking
- Steep

DIFFICULTY
- 1 2 3 4 5 +
less   more

San Gabriel Mountains

West Fork San Gabriel River 177

Oh-so-mellow when done on two wheels, the paved West Fork National Recreation Trail accompanies a year-round fishing stream the entire way. Here are twelve miles of the finest road biking in the L.A. region—and no car traffic to worry about.

East Fork San Gabriel River 181

Walk along (and sometimes through) the wildest tributary of the San Gabriel River, beneath canyon ramparts soaring thousands of feet. At trail's end, walk across the long-marooned "Bridge to Nowhere."

Cucamonga Peak 185

At nearly 9000 feet high, Cucamonga Peak stands sentinel-like only 4 miles from the edge of vast and rapidly growing Inland Empire region. The steep approach by way of cool, shady Icehouse Canyon challenges even fit hikers.

Old Baldy 189

No Southland hiker's roster of experiences is complete without the obligatory ascent of Mount San Antonio, or "Old Baldy." With a jump start via the Mount Baldy ski lift, the climb by foot becomes doable in a morning or an afternoon.

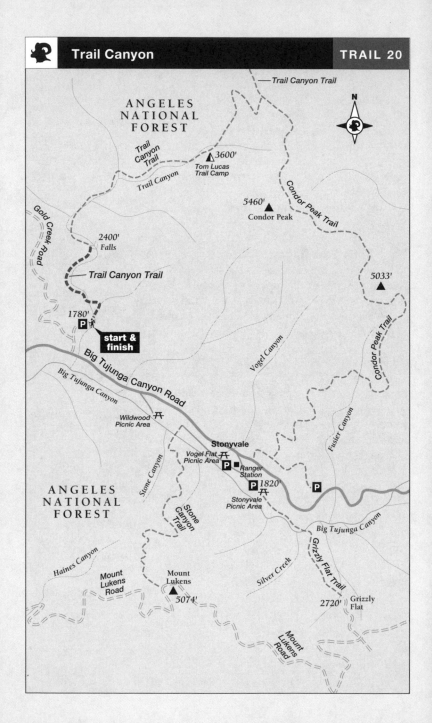

ANGELES
NATIONAL
FOREST

Trail Canyon Trail

N

Trail
Canyon
Trail

Trail Canyon Trail

3600'
Tom Lucas
Trail Camp

Condor Peak Trail

5460'
Condor Peak

Gold Creek Road

2400'
Falls

Trail Canyon Trail

5033'

1780'
P

start &
finish

Big Tujunga Canyon Road

Big Tujunga Canyon

Vogel Canyon

Wildwood
Picnic Area

Fusier Canyon

Stone Canyon

Stonyvale

Vogel Flat
Picnic Area
P
Ranger
Station

P 1820'

P

Stonyvale
Picnic Area

ANGELES
NATIONAL
FOREST

Stone
Canyon
Trail

Big Tujunga Canyon

Haines Canyon

Mount
Lukens
Road

Mount
Lukens

5074'

Silver Creek

Grizzly Flat Trail

2720'

Grizzly
Flat

Mount
Lukens
Road

Trail Canyon

When soaking rains come, Trail Canyon's normally indolent flow becomes a lively torrent. After tumbling through miles of rock-bound constrictions and sliding across many gently inclined declivities, the water comes to the lip of a real precipice. There the bubbly mixture momentarily attains weightlessness during a free fall of about 30 feet. This short, streamside hike takes you to a point overlooking those falls.

Best Time

Winter rains get the waterfall going nicely, starting around December or January. During winter flooding, the route may be impassable or hazardous due to high water. April is best for trailside wildflowers. By June or July most of the flowers have dried up and the flow of water at the falls slackens or stops.

Finding the Trail

From the foothill community of Sunland, off I-210, take either Oro Vista Ave. or Mt. Gleason Ave. north to Big Tujunga Canyon Road, and turn right. Some 5 miles up Big Tujunga Canyon, on the left (mile 2.0 according to highway mile markers), look for a dirt-road turnoff and (perhaps) a sign reading Trail Canyon Trail. Turn left (north) there, drive 0.2 mile uphill to a fork, go right, and descend 0.2 mile to an oak-shaded parking area on the right, just above Trail Canyon's melodious creek. A National Forest Adventure Pass is needed for parking.

TRAIL USE
Hike, Run
LENGTH
3.0 miles, 1½ hours
ELEVATION GAIN/LOSS
700'/700'
DIFFICULTY
– 1 **2** 3 4 5 +
TRAIL TYPE
Out & Back
SURFACE TYPE
Dirt

FEATURES
Permit Required
Dogs Allowed
Child Friendly
Canyon
Wildflowers
Birds
Wildlife
Cool & Shady
Great Views
Photo Opportunity
Camping
Historic
Geologic Interest

Trail Description

Beyond the parking lot, start up the trail (an old road)▶1 on foot, passing a few cabins and fording the creek for the first time. The now very deteriorated road goes on to follow an east tributary for a while, doubles back, contours around a ridge, and drops into **Trail Canyon** again (0.6 mile).▶2 The road ends there, and you continue up-canyon on a footpath. The path clings to the banks for 0.5 mile, crossing the stream several times, and then climbs the west wall▶3 to avoid a narrow, alder-choked section of the canyon. The falls come into view▶4 as you round a sharp bend, about 1.5 miles from the parking area.

■ **Waterfall**

Although many people have obviously done so, it's difficult and dangerous to slide down from the trail to the base of the falls. The falls can be reached by bushwhacking up the canyon from the point where the trail begins its ascent of the west wall; this might be fun scrambling for some during low water, but is hazardous during high water. Those sensitive to poison oak might also think twice about stepping off the trail.

▲ **Camping**

Backpacking is an option for those who wish to travel 4 miles up Trail Canyon to the cozy **Tom Lucas Trail Camp**, set in a grassy flat surrounded by oaks and jungle-like vegetation. The entire canyon, up to and a little beyond that point, is shaded by alders and other agreeable riparian vegetation.

🚶	MILESTONES
▶1	0.0 From parking lot, take Trail Canyon Trail, initially a disused road
▶2	0.6 Old road ends; narrow trail continues in canyon
▶3	1.1 Trail ascends canyon's left wall
▶4	1.5 Trail Canyon Falls comes into view

Trail Canyon Falls

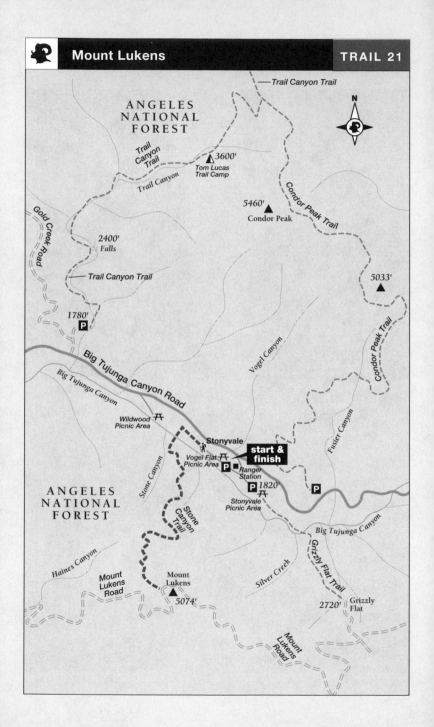

Mount Lukens

TRAIL 21

ANGELES
NATIONAL
FOREST

Trail Canyon Trail

Trail
Canyon
Trail

Trail Canyon Trail

Trail Canyon

△ 3600'
Tom Lucas
Trail Camp

5460' ▲
Condor Peak

Condor Peak Trail

N

Gold Creek Road

2400'
Falls

Trail Canyon Trail

5033'
▲

1780'
P

Big Tujunga Canyon Road

Big Tujunga Canyon

Vogel Canyon

Condor Peak Trail

Wildwood
Picnic Area

Stonyvale

Vogel Flat
Picnic Area
P

Ranger
Station

start &
finish

P 1820'

Stonyvale
Picnic Area

P

Foster Canyon

ANGELES
NATIONAL
FOREST

Stone Canyon

Stone
Canyon
Trail

Big Tujunga Canyon

Haines Canyon

Mount Lukens Road

Mount
Lukens
▲
5074'

Silver Creek

Grizzly Flat Trail

2720'

Grizzly
Flat

Mount
Lukens
Road

Mount Lukens

This grueling climb up the north slope of Mount Lukens is surely a walk on L.A.'s wild side. At the top you stand on the pinnacle (in elevation) of the City of Los Angeles, and peer over a vast urban plain.

Best Time

The cooler and clearer the weather, the better. December through February is usually best. Be aware that the hike begins and ends with a crossing of Big Tujunga Canyon's creek, which may swell to a dangerous width and depth after heavy rainfall, most likely during the winter. Save your lungs and avoid this hike during smoggy weather!

Finding the Trail

From the foothill community of Sunland, off I-210, take either Oro Vista Ave. or Mt. Gleason Ave. north to Big Tujunga Canyon Road. Turn right and drive east into the canyon. Some 7 miles up the canyon, look for the well-marked turnoff for Vogel Flat. Turn right, drive to the bottom of the hill, and park at **Vogel Flat Picnic Area**, open from 8 A.M. to 6 P.M. A short distance east is Stonyvale Picnic Area, open 6 A.M. to 10 P.M.—useful if you arrive early or will be returning late. A National Forest Adventure Pass is needed for parking.

Trail Description

On foot, head west down a narrow, paved road (private, but with public easement)►1 through the cabin

TRAIL USE
Hike
LENGTH
8.4 miles, 5 hours
ELEVATION GAIN/LOSS
3300'/3300'
DIFFICULTY
– 1 2 3 **4** 5 +
TRAIL TYPE
Out & Back
SURFACE TYPE
Dirt

FEATURES
Permits Required
Dogs Allowed
Mountain
Summit
Wildflowers
Great Views
Steep

View from Mount Lukens *across the ridges and peaks of the San Gabriels*

Mountain

community of **Stonyvale**. When the pavement ends after 0.7 mile, continue on dirt for another .25 mile or so. Choose a place to ford Big Tujunga creek,►2 step or wade across, and find the **Stone Canyon Trail** on the far bank. From afar you can spot this trail going straight up the sloping terrace just left (east) of Stone Canyon's wide, boulder-filled mouth. Once you're on the terrace, settle into a pace that will allow you to persevere over the next 3 miles and 3200 feet of vertical ascent.

From the vantage point of the first switchback, you can look down on the thousands of storm-tossed granitic boulders filling Stone Canyon from wall to wall. Ahead, there are many twists and turns along precipitous slopes covered by a thick blanket of chaparral. At or near ground level, a profusion of ferns, mosses, and herbaceous plants forms its own pygmy understory. Wildflowers scent the air during March and April.

Between 1.8 and 2.6 miles (from Vogel Flat), the trail hovers above an unnamed canyon to the east, nearly equal in drainage to Stone Canyon, but very steep and narrow. Down below you can often hear, and barely glimpse, an inaccessible waterfall. Long and short switchback segments take you rapidly higher to a steep, bulldozed track▶3 leading to the bald summit ridge of Mount Lukens. Go 0.5 mile farther, to the highest point on the ridge (4.2 miles),▶4 which is occupied by several antenna structures.

 Great Views

The summit lies within the city limit of Los Angeles, and is the highest point in any incorporated city in the county. The view, north and east across the various ridges and peaks of the San Gabriels, and south and west across the endlessly spreading city, can be fabulous—but only on a clear day.

大	**MILESTONES**

▶1	0.0 From Vogel Flat, head west on road through Stonyvale community
▶2	1.0 Ford Big Tujunga Canyon's creek; find lower end of Stone Canyon Trail
▶3	3.7 Narrow trail joins wider bulldozed path
▶4	4.2 Reach summit of Mount Lukens; return by the same route

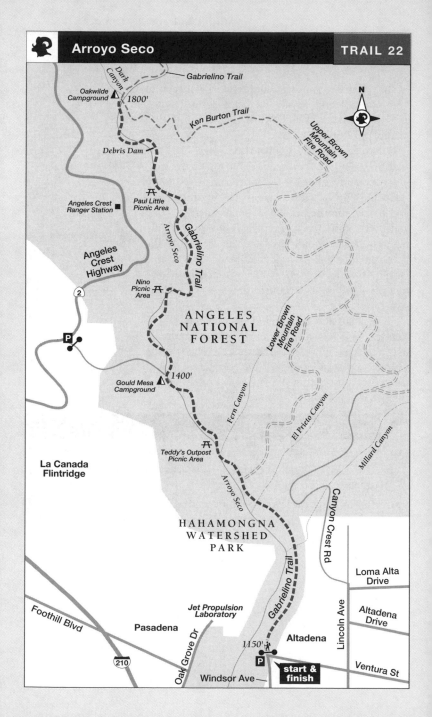

Gabrielino Trail

Dark Canyon

Oakwilde Campground ▲ 1800'

Ken Burton Trail

Debris Dam

Upper Brown Mountain Fire Road

N

Angeles Crest Ranger Station ■

Paul Little Picnic Area

Arroyo Seco

Gabrielino Trail

Angeles Crest Highway

2

Nino Picnic Area

ANGELES NATIONAL FOREST

Lower Brown Mountain Fire Road

P

Gould Mesa Campground ▲ 1400'

Fern Canyon

El Prieto Canyon

Millard Canyon

La Canada Flintridge

Teddy's Outpost Picnic Area

Arroyo Seco

HAHAMONGNA WATERSHED PARK

Canyon Crest Rd

Loma Alta Drive

Gabrielino Trail

Altadena Drive

Foothill Blvd

Jet Propulsion Laboratory

Pasadena

Oak Grove Dr

Lincoln Ave

210

1150'

Altadena

Ventura St

P

start & finish

Windsor Ave

Arroyo Seco

Arroyo Seco is a scenic treasure—all the more astounding when you consider that its exquisite sylvan glens and sparkling brook lie just 12-15 miles from L.A.'s city center. Often in the springtime, wildflower blooms splash color on nearly every sunstruck patch alongside the trail. If you haven't yet been freed from the notion that Los Angeles is nothing but a seething megalopolis, walk up the canyon of the Arroyo Seco. You'll be convinced otherwise! Several rest stops line the trail, making this a great route for a leisurely saunter, a speedy run, or a challenging bike ride.

Best Time

Short hikes into the Arroyo Seco are fine any time the air is clean. For the 10-mile round trip described here, a cooler day, or a cool time of day is preferred. Early morning is better, since by early afternoon tendrils of L.A. Basin smog often drift into the canyon.

Finding the Trail

Take the Windsor Ave./Arroyo Blvd. exit from Interstate 210, and drive 1 mile north on Windsor Ave. to where the street turns sharply right (east) and becomes Ventura St. The marked Gabrielino Trail going up Arroyo Seco starts here. Spacious free parking is available in a long narrow lot along the west side of Windsor Avenue, but it fills up fast on weekend mornings.

TRAIL USE
Hike, Run, Bike
LENGTH
10.0 miles, 4 hours
ELEVATION GAIN/LOSS
900'/900'
DIFFICULTY
– 1 2 **3** 4 5 +
TRAIL TYPE
Out & Back
SURFACE TYPE
Dirt

FEATURES
Permit Required
Dogs Allowed
Child Friendly
Handicap Access
Canyon
Streams
Waterfall
Autumn Colors
Wildflowers
Cool & Shady
Camping
Historic

Trail Description

The trail begins as a paved road ▸1 through Pasadena's **Hahamongna Watershed Park**, open sunrise to sunset only. At certain busy times on this lowermost stretch, you're likely to run into hikers cyclists, joggers, parents pushing strollers, and skateboarders—anything that moves without a motor.

Cool & Shady

Ahead, though, the going gets progressively rougher. Pavement yields to dirt with bridged stream crossings, then later the crossings become fords. Eventually, to the delight of purists, the route becomes merely a narrow trail. Sometimes even the trail disappears into the shallow water, sand, or rocks of the stream bed.

As you work your way up the canyon, you'll pass many old cabin sites and foundations. Some are conspicuously identified from afar by nonnative vegetation—eucalyptus, agaves, vinca, and so on—that might to a trained eye look totally out of place among the native flora. Some of the foundations are

Historic

associated with old resorts that thrived here before the completion of Angeles Crest Highway in the 1930s.

The Forest Service maintains several pleasant trailside rest stops: **Teddy's Outpost Picnic Area** at 1.9 miles, **Gould Mesa Campground** at 2.4 miles, ▸2 **Nino Picnic Area** at 3.0 miles, **Paul Little**

Shuttle Hike

OPTIONS

By means of a car shuttle, hikers and riders can traverse a 9.6-mile, downhill segment of the **Gabrielino Trail** from Switzers Picnic Area (off Angeles Crest Highway) to Pasadena. That traverse includes the scenic narrows section mentioned on p. 133.

Picnic Area at 4.0 miles, and **Oakwilde Campground▶4** at 5.0 miles. Just beyond Paul Little Picnic Area, the trail abruptly climbs the east wall of the canyon and later descends in a bypass maneuver around the large Brown Canyon Debris Dam.▶3 Otherwise, the trail is in or near the canyon bottom at all times.

Oakwilde Campground, which occupies the foundation remnants of the former Oak Wilde resort, is a great place for a picnic—as long as the warm-season gnats leave you alone. Head back on the same route when you're ready.

▲ Camping

Up-canyon from Oakwilde Campground, you can press on farther into perhaps the most gorgeous section of the Arroyo Seco canyon—a "narrows" flanked by soaring walls and dappled with shade cast by ever-present alders. Bigleaf maples put on a great show here in November, their bright yellow leaves boldly contrasting with the earthy greens, grays, and browns of the canyon's dimly lit bottom. This is a fun section for hikers, and quite technical for mountain bikers.

Although the lowermost (Pasadena) segment of the Gabrielino Trail is closed at night, there's 24-hour access to the middle stretch of the arroyo (on national forest land) by way of a service road that descends from Angeles Crest Highway in La Cañada to Gould Mesa Campground.

🚶	MILESTONES
▶1	0.0 Begin on pavement
▶2	2.4 Gould Mesa Campground (service road toward Angeles Crest Highway provides alternate access to or from the canyon)
▶3	4.2 Trail climbs high to bypass Brown Canyon Debris Dam
▶4	5.0 Oakwilde Campground; from here return by the same route

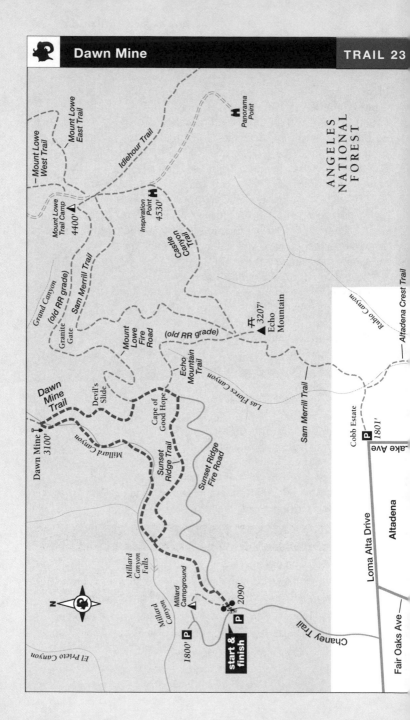

Panorama Point

ANGELES NATIONAL FOREST

Mount Lowe East Trail

Mount Lowe West Trail

Idlehour Trail

Inspiration Point 4530'

Mount Lowe Trail Camp 4400'

Castle Canyon Trail

Grand Canyon

Sam Merrill Trail

Granite Gate

(old RR grade)

Mount Lowe Fire Road

(old RR grade)

Echo Mountain 3207'

Dawn Mine Trail

Devil's Slide

Echo Mountain Trail

Cape of Good Hope

Las Flores Canyon

Dawn Mine 3100'

Millard Canyon

Sunset Ridge Trail

Sunset Ridge Fire Road

Sam Merrill Trail

Altadena Crest Trail

Rubio Canyon

Cobb Estate 1801'

P

Lake Ave

Loma Alta Drive

Altadena

Millard Canyon Falls

Millard Campground

Millard Canyon

El Prieto Canyon

N

1800'

P

2090'

P

start & finish

Chaney Trail

Fair Oaks Ave

Dawn Mine

Millard Canyon's happily splashing stream, presided over by oaks, alders, maples, and bigcone Douglas-firs, is the main attraction on this hike. You can also snoop around the site of the Dawn Mine, one of the more promising gold prospects in the San Gabriels, worked intermittently from 1895 until the 1950s.

Best Time

October through May is best. An early start is good any time. That way you'll have shade during the climbing phase, and you'll be assured of a parking place at the trailhead, which is popular with mountain bikers and hikers.

Finding the Trail

Take the Lincoln Ave. exit from Interstate 210, drive 2 miles north on Lincoln to Loma Alta Drive, turn right, go 0.6 mile east, and look for the obscurely marked, narrow paved road on the left signed **Chaney Trail**. You'll pass a sturdy gate, open 6 A.M. to 10 P.M. Continue uphill to the top of Sunset Ridge, where you'll find limited parking at the road summit. This is the preferred trailhead. Additional parking is available farther on near Millard Campground. A National Forest Adven-ture Pass is needed for parking in both places.

Trail Description

Walk east on the gated, paved **Sunset Ridge fire road.** ▶1 After about 100 yards, pass a foot trail on

TRAIL USE
Hike
LENGTH
5.6 miles, 3.5 hours
ELEVATION GAIN/LOSS
1600'/1600'
DIFFICULTY
– 1 2 **3** 4 5 +
TRAIL TYPE
Loop
SURFACE TYPE
Dirt

FEATURES
Permit Required
Dogs Allowed
Canyon
Autumn Colors
Cool & Shady
Secluded
Historic

Mining machinery

 Canyon

the left leading down to **Millard Campground**. Continue another 300 yards to a second foot trail on the left (**Sunset Ridge Trail**).▶2 Take it. On it you contour north and east along Millard Canyon's south wall, passing above the 50-foot-high **Millard Canyon Falls**.

You begin climbing in earnest at about 0.7 mile and soon reach a trail fork.▶3 The left branch (your return route) goes down 100 yards, past a private cabin, to the canyon bottom. You go right, uphill. Switchbacks long and short take you farther up along the pleasantly shaded canyon wall to an intersection with **Sunset Ridge fire road** (2.3 miles)▶4, just below a rocky knob called **Cape of Good Hope**.

Turn left on the fire road, and walk past the Cape of Good Hope. The trail to **Echo Mountain**, intersecting on the right, and the fire road ahead are both part of the original Mt. Lowe Railway bed (see Trail 24, p. 139)—now a self-guiding historical trail. Continue your ascent on the fire road/railway bed to post No. 4 on the left (2.8 miles).▶5 There you'll find a trail descending to **Dawn Mine** in Millard Canyon. This is a reworked, primitive version of the

---

Trail Running

OPTIONS

Much of the Dawn Mine loop route, as described above, is not easily runnable due to its sometimes sketchy nature. By taking the paved (but closed to auto traffic) Sunset Ridge fire road instead of the Sunset Ridge Trail, you can run the initial stretch without worrying about tripping.

While you're in the area, consider visiting **Millard Falls** if there's a decent flow of water in Millard Canyon. A short trail leads from Millard Campground to base of the falls.

mule path once used to haul ore from the mine to the railway above. On the way down you may encounter a dicey passage or two across perpetually sliding talus.

After reaching the gloomy canyon bottom (3.4 miles),►**6** the trail goes upstream along the east bank for about 100 yards to the long abandoned Dawn Mine, perched on the west-side slope. The gaping entrance to the lower shaft may seem inviting to explore, but it could collapse without warning.

From the mine, head down-canyon past crystalline mini-pools, the flotsam and jetsam of the mining days, and storm-tossed boulders. Much of the original trail in the canyon has been washed away, but a new generation of hikers has beaten down a pretty good semblance of a path.

Cool & Shady

After swinging around an abrupt bend to the right, the canyon becomes dark and gloomy once again. After another 0.5 mile you'll come to the aforementioned trail climbing up to the left.►**7** Pass the private cabin and hook up with the Sunset Ridge Trail,►**8** which will take you back to the Sunset Ridge fire road and your car.►**10**

🚶 MILESTONES

►**1**	0.0 From parking area at crest of Chaney Trail, follow paved Sunset Ridge fire road uphill
►**2**	0.2 Turn left on Sunset Ridge Trail
►**3**	0.8 At trail fork bear right (uphill), staying on Sunset Ridge Trail
►**4**	2.3 Turn left when you reach Sunset Ridge fire road
►**5**	2.8 Go left on the narrow trail that descends toward Dawn Mine
►**6**	3.4 Reach Millard Canyon bottom; visit Dawn Mine, just upstream, then proceed down the canyon
►**7**	4.7 Find and follow trail ascending left out of the canyon
►**8**	4.8 Join Sunset Ridge Trail; stay right
►**9**	5.6 Arrive back at Chaney Trail parking area

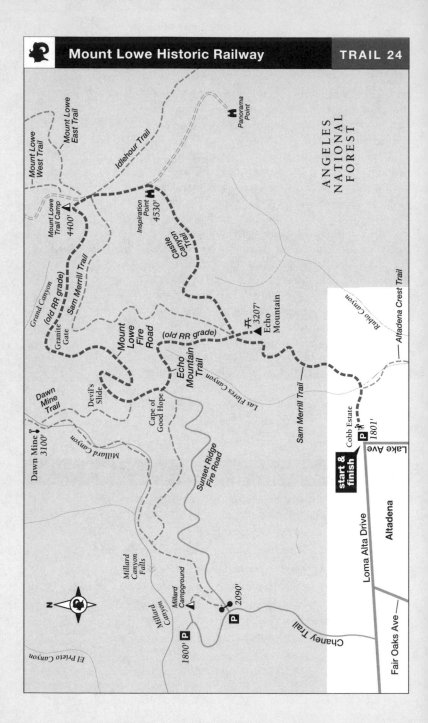

Mount Lowe West Trail

Mount Lowe East Trail

Idlehour Trail

Panorama Point

ANGELES NATIONAL FOREST

Mount Lowe Trail Camp 4400'

Inspiration Point 4530'

Castle Canyon Trail

Grand Canyon (old RR grade)

Sam Merrill Trail

Granite Gate

Mount Lowe Fire Road

(old RR grade)

Echo Mountain 3207'

Echo Mountain Trail

Las Flores Canyon

Rubio Canyon

Altadena Crest Trail

Dawn Mine Trail

Devil's Slide

Cape of Good Hope

Dawn Mine 3100'

Millard Canyon

Sunset Ridge Fire Road

Sam Merrill Trail

Cobb Estate

start & finish

1801'

Lake Ave

Loma Alta Drive

Altadena

Millard Canyon Falls

Millard Campground

Millard Canyon

2090'

1800'

El Prieto Canyon

N

Chaney Trail

Fair Oaks Ave

Mount Lowe Historic Railway

An engineering marvel when built in the 1890s, the Mount Lowe Railway has lived a checkered past full of glory and destruction. Before its final abandonment in the mid-1930s, the line carried over 3 million touring passengers. Tourists ascended in three stages: 1) a trolley from Altadena into lower Rubio Canyon; 2) an incline railway gaining 1300 feet of elevation up the side of Rubio Canyon to Echo Mountain; and 3) a mountain trolley that climbed another 1200 vertical feet along airy slopes to "Ye Alpine Tavern," the end of the line. Of all the various ways to approach and follow the old rail route today, the trail route described here is the most complete and comprehensive.

Best Time

Since most of the route is exposed to the sun, pick a cool day from November through April. Otherwise, you'd better get a very early start.

Finding the Trail

The trailhead lies on the grounds of the long-demolished Cobb Estate, at the intersection of Lake Ave. and Loma Alta Drive in Altadena—3.6 miles north of Interstate 210 via Lake Avenue. Free curbside parking is abundant in the neighborhood.

Trail Description

Walk east past the stone pillars at the Cobb Estate entrance▶1 and continue 150 yards on a narrow,

TRAIL USE
Hike, Run

LENGTH
11.4 miles, 6 hours

ELEVATION GAIN/LOSS
2800'/2800'

DIFFICULTY
− 1 2 3 **4** 5 +

TRAIL TYPE
Loop

SURFACE TYPE
Dirt

FEATURES
Dogs Allowed
Mountain
Wildflowers
Great Views
Photo Opportunity
Historic
Moonlight Hiking

blacktop driveway. The driveway bends left, but you keep walking straight (east). Soon you come to a water fountain on the rim of Las Flores Canyon and a sign indicating the start of the **Sam Merrill Trail.▶2** This trail goes left over the top of a small debris dam and begins a switchback ascent of Las Flores Canyon's precipitous east wall, while another trail (the Altadena Crest equestrian trail) veers to the right, down the canyon.

The 2.5 miles of steady ascent on the Sam Merrill Trail may seem to go by rather quickly and enjoyably, especially if the day is clear enough to see much of the L.A. Basin and the ocean. Turn right when you get to the top of the grade and walk south over to **Echo Mountain,▶3** which is more like the shoulder of a ridge. Here you'll find a historical plaque and some picnic tables, near a grove of incense cedars and bigleaf maples. Perched on Echo Mountain during the railroad's early days (late 1890s) was "The White City," featuring two hotels, a small zoo, the brightest searchlight in the world, and an observatory. All structures were either heavily damaged or burned in windstorms and wildfires during the early 1900s.

Poke around and you'll find many foundation ruins and piles of concrete rubble. An old "bull-wheel" and cables for the incline railway were thoughtfully left behind after the Forest Service cleared away what remained of the buildings here in the 1950s and '60s.

Historic

Your self-guiding historical tour of the railroad grade begins now, on the signed **Echo Mountain Trail,▶4** where you'll walk over railroad ties still imbedded in the ground. Here are historical tidbits linked to the posted "stations" along way (numbers in parentheses refer to hiking mileage starting from Echo Mountain):

Station 1 (0.0) Echo Mountain.

Station 2 (0.5) View of Circular Bridge. You can't see it from here, but passengers at this point first noticed the 400-foot-diameter circular bridge (Station 6) jutting from the slope above. As you walk on ahead, you'll notice the many concrete footings, which supported trestles bridging the side ravines of Las Flores Canyon.

Station 3 (0.8) Cape of Good Hope. You're now at the junction of the Echo Mountain Trail and Sunset Ridge fire road.►5 The tracks swung in a 200-degree arc around the rocky promontory just west—Cape of Good Hope. North of this dizzying passage, riders were treated to the longest stretch of straight track—only 225 feet long. The entire original line from Echo Mountain to Ye Alpine Tavern had 127 curves and 114 straight sections.

Great Views

Station 4 (1.0) Dawn Station/ Devil's Slide. Dawn Mine lies below in Millard Canyon. Gold-bearing ore, packed up by mules from the canyon bottom, was loaded onto the train here. Ahead lay a treacherous stretch of crumbling granite, the Devil's Slide, which was eventually bridged by a trestle.

Station 5 (1.2) Horseshoe Curve. Just beyond this station, Horseshoe Curve enabled the railway to gain elevation above Millard Canyon. The grade just beyond Horseshoe Curve was 7 percent—steepest on the mountain segment of the line.

Station 6 (1.6) Circular Bridge. An engineering accomplishment of worldwide fame, the Circular Bridge carried passengers into midair over the upper walls of Las Flores Canyon. Look for the concrete supports of this bridge down along the chaparral-covered slopes to the right.

Station 7 (2.0) Horseshoe Curve Overview. Passengers here looked down on Horseshoe Curve,

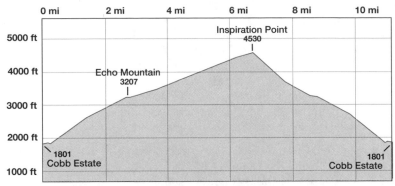

	0 mi	2 mi	4 mi	6 mi	8 mi	10 mi

Inspiration Point
4530

Echo Mountain
3207

1801
Cobb Estate

1801
Cobb Estate

5000 ft

4000 ft

3000 ft

2000 ft

1000 ft

TRAIL 24 Mount Lowe Historic Railway Elevation Profile

and could also see all three levels of steep, twisting track climbing the east wall of Millard Canyon.

 Great Views

Station 8 (2.4) Granite Gate. A narrow slot blasted out of solid granite on a sheer north-facing slope, Granite Gate took eight months to cut. Look for the electric wire support dangling from the rock above.

Station 9 (3.4) Ye Alpine Tavern. ▶6 The tavern, which later became a fancy hotel, was located at Crystal Springs, the source that still provides water (which needs purification) for backpackers staying overnight at today's Mount Lowe Trail Camp. The rails never got farther than here, although it was hoped they would one day reach the summit of Mount Lowe, 1200 feet higher.

Night Hiking

Night use of the Sunset Ridge and Sam Merrill approaches is unrestricted (except that the access to Sunset Ridge closes at 10 P.M.). Hiking the railroad grade on a clear night lit by a full moon can be wonderful. Remember to bring a flashlight; the bright glare of city lights in your eyes may make it difficult to see the trail beneath your feet.

OPTIONS

Station 10 (3.9) Inspiration Point.►7 From Ye Alpine Tavern, tourists could saunter over to Inspiration Point along part of the never-finished rail extension to Mt. Lowe. Sighting tubes (still in place today) helped visitors locate places of interest below. A beautiful open-air pavilion stands here, replacing an earlier shelter dating from the early 1900s.

Inspiration Point is the last station on the self-guiding trail. The fastest and easiest way to make the return descent is by way of the **Castle Canyon Trail**, which starts directly below Inspiration Point. After 2 miles you'll arrive back on the old railway grade just north of Echo Mountain.►8 Retrace your steps on the Sam Merrill Trail.

The route described above is not suitable for the average mountain biker, mainly due to the steep and narrow initial and concluding segment on the Sam Merrill Trail. If you access the upper railway grade by way of the **Sunset Ridge fire road**, though, you'll enjoy one of the best nontechnical mountain-bike treks in the Southland.

 **Mountain Biking**

🚶	MILESTONES
►1	0.0 Walk east through grounds of Cobb Estate
►2	0.2 Follow the Sam Merrill Trail from canyon-rim trailhead
►3	2.7 Arrive at Echo Mtn. historic site; explore ruins to the south
►4	2.8 Follow self-guiding Mt. Lowe Railway tour, heading north
►5	3.6 Reach Sunset Ridge Fire Road; turn right
►6	6.2 Pass Mt. Lowe Trail Camp, former Ye Alpine Tavern
►7	6.7 Inspiration Point; enjoy the view, then follow Castle Canyon Trail downhill toward Echo Mtn.
►8	8.7 Rejoin Sam Merrill Trail; descend toward Cobb Estate
►9	11.2 Arrive at Cobb Estate trailhead on the canyon rim

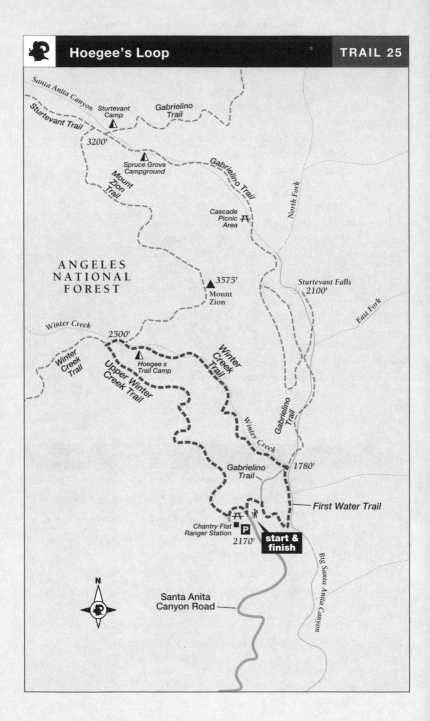

Santa Anita Canyon

Sturtevant Trail

Sturtevant Camp

Gabrielino Trail

3200'

Spruce Grove Campground

Mount Zion Trail

Gabrielino Trail

North Fork

Cascade Picnic Area

ANGELES NATIONAL FOREST

3575'
Mount Zion

Sturtevant Falls 2100'

East Fork

Winter Creek

2500'

Winter Creek Trail

Hoegee's Trail Camp

Upper Winter Creek Trail

Winter Creek Trail

Gabrielino Trail

Winter Creek

1780'

Gabrielino Trail

First Water Trail

Chantry Flat Ranger Station

P

2170'

start & finish

Big Santa Anita Canyon

N

Santa Anita Canyon Road

Hoegee's Loop

The canyons of Big Santa Anita and Winter Creek exist in a time warp. On foot is the only way in for the owners of the 82 cabins on Forest Service land here, dating from the early 1900s. Typical cabin amenities include kerosene lamps, drinking water carried in by the jugful, and one-hole privies. The following tour on rustic trails takes you through both of these secluded canyons, where trickling streams and rustling leaves make you forget you're anywhere near a big city.

Best Time

Any time of year is fine for traveling the well-shaded route. Try to avoid the smog, which can sneak into the canyons during the afternoon.

Finding the Trail

From Interstate 210 in Arcadia, follow Santa Anita Ave. north. Continue to the edge of the city, pass a sturdy gate (open 6 A.M. to 10 P.M.), and ascend along a curling and precipitous ribbon of asphalt to your destination at the end of the road: **Chantry Flat**. Spacious (but often inadequate) parking lots, a ranger station, a picnic ground, and a mom-and-pop concession stand are here. A National Forest Adventure Pass is required for parking in the public lots. Additional parking space may be available through the concession stand.

TRAIL USE
Hike, Run
LENGTH
5.3 miles, 2.5 hours
ELEVATION GAIN/LOSS
1300'/1300'
DIFFICULTY
– 1 **2** 3 4 5 +
TRAIL TYPE
Loop
SURFACE TYPE
Dirt

FEATURES
Permit Required
Dogs Allowed
Canyon
Streams
Waterfall
Autumn Colors
Cool & Shady
Camping
Historic

Trail Description

The concession at Chantry Flat includes an unusual freight business—the last pack station operating year round in California. Almost daily, horses, mules and burros carry building materials and other supplies to canyon residents.

Start at the south edge of the lower parking lot at Chantry Flat,►1 where a gated, paved road (the easternmost leg of the Gabrielino Trail) starts descending into Big Santa Anita Canyon. After rounding the first sharp bend, 0.2 mile down, veer right onto an obscure trail,►2 known as the **First Water Trail**. Descend on precipitous switchbacks (watch your step!) to the stream below,►3 where an appropriately named First Water Camp welcomed hot and footsore hikers in the 1920s and '30s.

Turn left (upstream) and follow the rudiments of a trail amid streamside cabins and boulders to the confluence of Big Santa Anita Canyon and **Winter Creek,►4**, at the foot of the paved section of the **Gabrielino Trail**. The main Gabrielino Trail goes north into upper Big Santa Anita Canyon, but you head west into the steep-walled confines of **Winter Creek**. The well-traveled trail snakes upward, sometimes along the stream, otherwise up on the canyon walls in order to bypass flood-control dams and various cabins.

The serenely beautiful **Big Santa Anita/Winter Creek confluence** is the historical setting for Roberts' Camp, a thriving resort during the early 1900s. During the peak of its popularity, a branch of the L.A. County Library and a post office were established here to serve guests and passing hikers.

▲ Camping

After traveling 1.5 miles from the confluence, you come to **Hoegee's Trail Camp,►5** tucked into a shady nook on Winter Creek's south bank. Nearby are the scattered foundation ruins of Hoegee's Camp (later called Camp Ivy), a hiker's resort established in 1908, and destroyed by wildfire in 1953. Today, Hoegee's is one of the more popular trail camps in the San Gabriels—charming, rustic, and relatively easy to reach.

Nearby Trails

A plethora of possibilities awaits the ambitious traveler starting out from Chantry Flat. **Sturtevant Falls** in upper Big Santa Anita Canyon is a popular (often too popular) out-and-back destination in spring and early summer. Many hikers go farther, completing either the 9.4-mile **Mount Zion loop**, or a challenging 13.8-mile loop over the summit of Mount Wilson.

Your looping return is by way of the Upper Winter Creek Trail. From Hoegee's, continue upstream on the north bank, passing the Mt. Zion Trail on the right. The trail swings left, crosses the stream, and climbs obliquely up Winter Creek's south canyon wall. In a short while you reach a signed junction.▶6 The trail on the right goes toward Mount Wilson. You take the left trail, which takes you back to your starting point▶7 2.6 miles away on a curving, gently undulating course.

 Historic

🚶 MILESTONES

▶1   0.0   Follow Gabrielino Trail (paved service road) downhill

▶2   0.2   Turn right on obscure First Water Trail

▶3   0.6   Reach Big Santa Anita Canyon bottom; turn upstream

▶4   1.0   Reach confluence of Big Santa Anita Canyon and Winter Creek; follow Winter Creek Trail upstream

▶5   2.5   Pass Hoegee's Camp; continue upstream, staying left

▶6   2.7   Trail junction; trail to Mount Wilson goes right; you stay left

▶7   5.3   Return to Chantry Flat

ANGELES
NATIONAL
FOREST

1800'

Monrovia Canyon Falls

Monrovia Canyon

MONROVIA
CANYON
PARK

Nature
Center

P

start &
finish

Sawpit Canyon

1350'

P

Sawpit
Canyon
Reservoir

Sawpit
Canyon
Fire Road

Park Entrance

P

Canyon Boulevard

Sawpit Canyon

Monrovia

N

Monrovia Falls

Tucked away in two shady canyons behind the foothill community of Monrovia is one of the most beautiful parks in the Los Angeles area: Monrovia Canyon Park. Adding spice to the rich riparian vegetation in both canyons is 40-foot-high Monrovia Canyon Falls, which runs with bubbly exuberance for weeks or months after the rainy season ends.

Best Time

The only thing that can spoil this superb little outing is dirty air. Avoid going on a smoggy day. The park is closed every Tuesday.

Finding the Trail

Exit Interstate 210 in Monrovia at Myrtle Ave. and drive north for 1.9 miles to its end at Scenic Drive. Turn right and follow Scenic Drive on a meandering eastward course for three blocks, then keep straight as Canyon Boulevard joins from the right. Proceed uphill on **Canyon Blvd.**, which crookedly ascends alongside a dry riverbed to the park entrance, open 8 A.M. to 5 P.M. Pay a small day-use fee here, and drive an additional 0.5 mile to the road's end, where you'll find picnic tables, a nature center, and the hiking trail going up Monrovia Canyon. ▶1

Trail Description

The trail following the canyon mostly sticks close to the sparkling stream. Sometimes the trail gets narrow, eroded, and slippery enough to cause some

TRAIL USE
Hike
LENGTH
1.6 miles, 1 hour
ELEVATION GAIN/LOSS
500'/500'
DIFFICULTY
– **1** 2 3 4 5 +
TRAIL TYPE
Out & Back
SURFACE TYPE
Dirt

FEATURES
Dogs Allowed
Child Friendly
Canyon
Streams
Waterfall
Autumn Colors
Cool & Shady

Cool & Shady

difficulty with footing—a cautionary note for those with small kids. You ascend moderately the entire distance. Alder, oak, and bay trees cluster in the canyon bottom so densely that hardly any sunlight is admitted, even at midday.

After 0.8 mile the sound of splashing water heralds your arrival at the falls,►2 where the stream either leaps or dribbles down two distinct declivities on a water-worn cliff face.

There's only one reasonable way to return—the way you came.

MILESTONES

►1	0.0 Follow trail up Monrovia Canyon from picnic area next to nature center
►2	0.8 Trail ends at foot of Monrovia Canyon Falls; retrace your steps
►3	1.6 Arrive back at nature center

Monrovia Canyon Falls

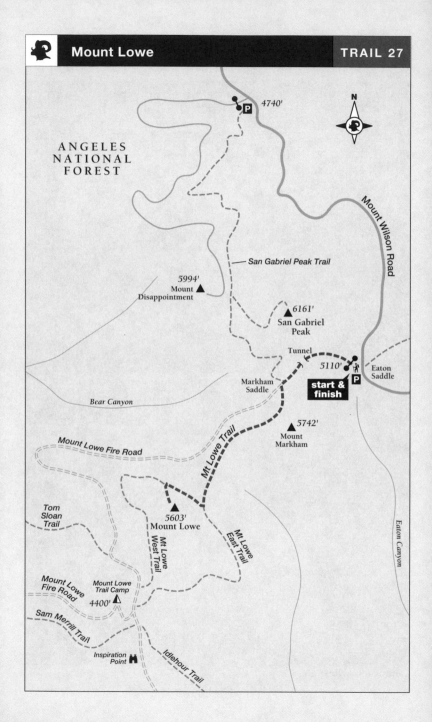

**ANGELES
NATIONAL
FOREST**

4740'

N

San Gabriel Peak Trail

5994'
Mount
Disappointment

6161'
San Gabriel
Peak

Tunnel

5110'

Eaton
Saddle

Markham
Saddle

**start &
finish**

Bear Canyon

5742'
Mount
Markham

Mt Lowe Trail

Mount Lowe Fire Road

Tom
Sloan
Trail

5603'
Mount Lowe

*Mt Lowe
West Trail*

*Mt Lowe
East Trail*

Eaton Canyon

Mount
Lowe
Fire Road

Mount Lowe
Trail Camp

4400'

Sam Merrill Trail

Inspiration
Point

Idlehour Trail

Mount Wilson Road

Mount Lowe

Mount Lowe, the never-reached destination of the Mount Lowe Railway (see Trail 24, p. 139), isn't the highest peaklet in the front range of the San Gabriel Mountains, but it does offer a superb and comprehensive view of the valleys below. This is the easy route to the top, approaching the summit from Mount Wilson Road via the peak's "back" side.

TRAIL USE
Hike, Run
LENGTH
3.2 miles, 1½ hours
ELEVATION GAIN/LOSS
500'/500'
DIFFICULTY
– 1 **2** 3 4 5 +
TRAIL TYPE
Out & Back
SURFACE TYPE
Dirt

FEATURES
Permit Required
Dogs Allowed
Mountain
Summit
Great Views
Moonlight Hiking

Best Time

Clean-air days are preferred, any time of year. Snow can cling to the steep, north side of Mount Lowe for several days after a winter storm, creating a possibly hazardous trail condition in a couple of spots.

Finding the Trail

From Interstate 210 in **La Cañada**, drive 14 miles north on Angeles Crest Highway to Red Box Station. Turn right on Mount Wilson Road and proceed exactly 2.4 miles to a roadside parking area at unmarked Eaton Saddle. This small, but popular trailhead could be jammed with cars on the weekends. Don't forget to display your National Forest Adventure Pass.

Trail Description

Walk past the gate on the west side of Mount Wilson Road and proceed up the dirt road▶1 (**Mount Lowe Fire Road**) that curves under the precipitous south face of San Gabriel Peak. As you approach a short tunnel,▶2 (0.3 mile) dating from 1942, look for the remnants of a cliff-hanging trail to the left of the tunnel's east entrance.

At **Markham Saddle** (0.5 mile) the fire road starts to descend slightly—don't continue on the road. Instead, find the **Mount Lowe Trail** on the left (south).►3 You contour southwest above the fire road for about 0.6 mile, and then start climbing across the east flank of Mount Lowe without much change of direction.

At 1.3 miles, make a sharp right turn►4 (the Mount Lowe east trail goes straight). Proceed 0.2 mile uphill, then go left on a short spur trail►5 to reach the barren summit.►6

 Great Views

Late in the year, when the smog lightens, but temperatures still hover within a moderate register, come up to Mt. Lowe to toast the setting sun. When it's time to go, return the way you came.

Historic

During the Mount Lowe Railway's heyday, thousands of tourists disembarked at the "tavern" below and tramped Mount Lowe's east- and west-side trails for a better view of the lowlands. Some reminders of that era remain on the Mount Lowe west trail: Volunteers have repainted, relettered, and returned to their proper places some of the many sighting tubes that helped the early tourists familiarize themselves with the surrounding geography. The optional loop around Mount Lowe's west and east trails adds another 2 miles to your journey.

MILESTONES

►1	0.0	From Eaton Saddle, follow Mt. Lowe Fire Road west
►2	0.3	Pass through tunnel
►3	0.5	Leave fire road; take Mt. Lowe Trail on the left
►4	1.3	Turn right on Mt. Lowe west trail
►5	1.5	Turn left on spur trail to summit
►6	1.6	Mt. Lowe summit; return by the same route
►7	3.2	Arrive back at Eaton Saddle

Summit of Mount Lowe

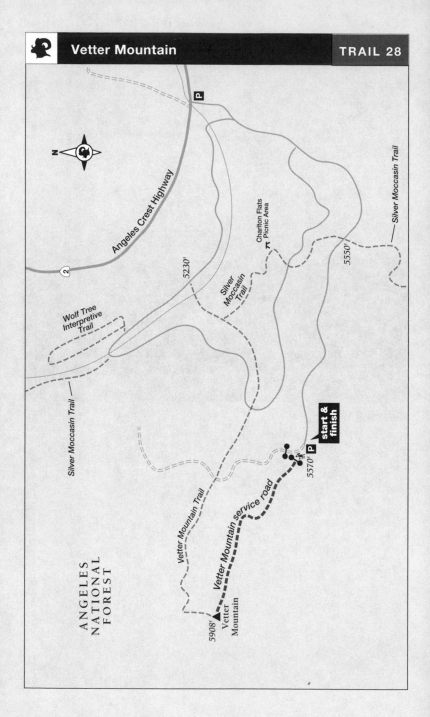

N

Angeles Crest Highway

2

P

Silver Moccasin Trail

Charlton Flats
Picnic Area

5230'

Silver
Moccasin
Trail

5550'

Wolf Tree
Interpretive
Trail

Silver Moccasin Trail

start &
finish

P

5570'

Vetter Mountain Trail

Vetter Mountain service road

ANGELES
NATIONAL
FOREST

5908'
Vetter
Mountain

Vetter Mountain

Vetter Mountain's pint-sized fire-lookout building, perched on a rounded summit nearly devoid of vegetation, takes advantage of a 360-degree view over the midsection of the San Gabriels. The lookout reopened for service in 1998 after an 18-year hiatus. The facility is staffed on weekends and on some weekdays during the fire season (summer and fall). The public is welcome to hike to the summit anytime.

Best Time

All year is fine, though the access road to the trailhead may be blocked by snow in winter.

Finding the Trail

From Interstate 210 in La Cañada, drive 23 miles up Angeles Crest Highway to the **Charlton Flats Picnic Area** (at mile 47.5, according to the roadside milemarkers). Turn left into the picnic area (open 6 A.M. to 10 P.M.) and stay left at all road forks until you reach a gate where the dirt access road to the Vetter Lookout begins. A National Forest Adventure Pass is required for parking.

Trail Description

Go past the vehicle gate and head moderately uphill on the access road,►1 going all the way to the 5908-foot summit of Vetter Mountain.►2 Steps lead to the low lookout structure. Compared to most fire lookouts, this one appears to have lost its legs.

Peering north and east from the lookout, you'll

TRAIL USE
Hike, Run
LENGTH
1.4 miles, 1 hour
ELEVATION GAIN/LOSS
350'/350'
DIFFICULTY
– **1** 2 3 4 5 +
TRAIL TYPE
Out & Back
SURFACE TYPE
Dirt

FEATURES
Permit Required
Dogs Allowed
Child Friendly
Mountain
Summit
Birds
Wildflowers
Great Views
Historic
Moonlight Hiking

Great Views

spot Pacifico Mountain, Mt. Williamson, Waterman Mountain, Twin Peaks, Old Baldy, and other summits of the San Gabriel Mountains "High Country." The Front Range of the San Gabriels sprawls west and south, blocking from view most of the L.A. cityscape.

Aside from visiting the lookout, spend some time poking around **Charlton Flats'** heterogeneous forest of live oak, Coulter pine, Jeffrey pine, sugar pine, incense cedar, and bigcone Douglas-fir. With binoculars, a bird book, and a wildflower guide, you and your kids can take your sweet time, stopping as you please to admire a soaring hawk or raven, a noisy acorn woodpecker or Steller's jay, or an unfamiliar plant in bloom.

Birds

Return the same way you came.

On Mt. Vetter, as elsewhere, on the higher and drier slopes of the San Gabriels the toll of the 1998-2002 drought is apparant. Bark beetles have fatally attacked many of the trees, which for lack of enough sap have been unable to defend themselves.

MILESTONES

▶1	0.0	Follow dirt access road uphill to Vetter Mountain summit
▶2	0.7	Arrive at Vetter Mountain summit; return by the same route
▶3	1.4	Return to foot of access road

Vetter Mountain Lookout

Vetter Mountain

Vetter Mountain can also be reached by way of the Vetter Mountain Trail. It starts at the lowermost part of Charlton Flats Picnic Area, and ascends 1.3 miles to the uppermost part of the lookout access road.

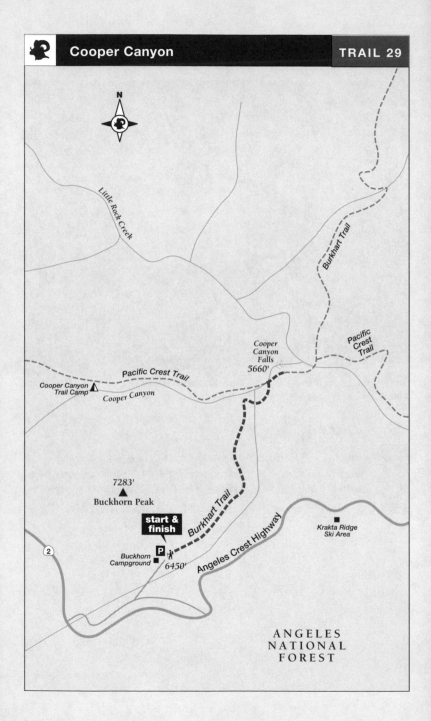

N

Little Rock Creek

Burkhart Trail

Pacific Crest Trail

Cooper Canyon Falls 5660'

Pacific Crest Trail

Cooper Canyon Trail Camp

Cooper Canyon

7283' Buckhorn Peak

start & finish

Burkhart Trail

Krakta Ridge Ski Area

2

Buckhorn Campground

6450'

Angeles Crest Highway

ANGELES NATIONAL FOREST

Cooper Canyon

Cooper Canyon Falls roars with the melting snows of early spring, then settles down to a quiet whisper by June or July. You can cool off in the spray of the 25-foot cascade, or at least sit on a water-smoothed log and soak your feet in the chilly, alder-shaded pool just below the base of the falls. Following your descent to the falls, you'll need to climb back up—but the high-country forest is dense enough to offer shade for a comfortable return.

Best Time

April (snow-cover allowing) through July are best. Autumn has it own pleasures, though the canyon may run dry by then. Angeles Crest Highway, which leads to the trailhead, often closes in winter at higher elevations due to snow or landslides.

Finding the Trail

From Interstate 210 in La Cañada, drive 34 miles up Angeles Crest Highway to the Buckhorn Campground entrance road (mile 58.3, according to the roadside mile-markers). Drive all the way through the campground to the far (northeast) end, where a short stub of dirt road leads to the Burkhart trailhead. You must display a National Forest Adventure Pass.

Trail Description

Follow the **Burkhart Trail,**▶1 which takes off down the west wall of an unnamed ravine leading to

TRAIL USE
Hike, Run
LENGTH
3.0 miles, 1.5 hours
ELEVATION GAIN/LOSS
800'/800'
DIFFICULTY
– 1 **2** 3 4 5 +
TRAIL TYPE
Out & Back
SURFACE TYPE
Dirt

FEATURES
Permit Required
Dogs Allowed
Child Friendly
Canyon
Stream
Waterfall
Birds
Wildlife
Cool & Shady
Photo Opportunity
Secluded

Falls in Cooper Canyon

Cooper Canyon Trail Camp

OPTIONS

From the Burkhart Trail's intersection with the Pacific Crest Trail, backpackers can travel west 1.2 miles to Cooper Canyon Trail Camp, one of the nicest overnight destinations in the San Gabriels.

Cooper Canyon. In spring the ravine bottom is garnished by two thin waterfalls, both off to the right and partially visible from the trail. The first, a little gem of a cascade, drops 10 feet into a rock grotto near the trail. The second, 30 feet high, is a bit farther away and difficult and dangerous to approach.

At 1.2 miles, the trail bends east to follow Cooper Canyon's south bank.►2 Continue another 0.3 mile, down past the junction of the trail (**Pacific Crest Trail**) ►3 that doubles back to follow the north bank upstream. Look or listen for water plunging over the rocky declivity to the left. A rough pathway leads down off the trail to the alder-fringed pool below.

Miles of fine high-country hiking trails fan out from Cooper Canyon. The Pacific Crest Trail rambles east and west, more or less sticking with the Angeles Crest, and the Burkhart Trail climbs north over a ridge and descends toward the Devil's Punchbowl in the "High Desert"—the rim of the Mojave Desert. Trail 32, on p. 173, traverses the northernmost segment of the Burkhart Trail, starting at Devil's Punchbowl Natural Area.

In the right season (April or May most years) the falls in Cooper Canyon are one of the best unheralded attractions of the San Gabriel Mountains.

	MILESTONES
►1	0.0 Take Burkhart Trail downslope from trailhead
►2	1.2 Trail bends right to follow bottom of Cooper Canyon
►3	1.5 Pacific Crest Trail joins from the left; Cooper Canyon Falls is just ahead, on the left
►4	3.0 After returning the same way, arrive back at trailhead

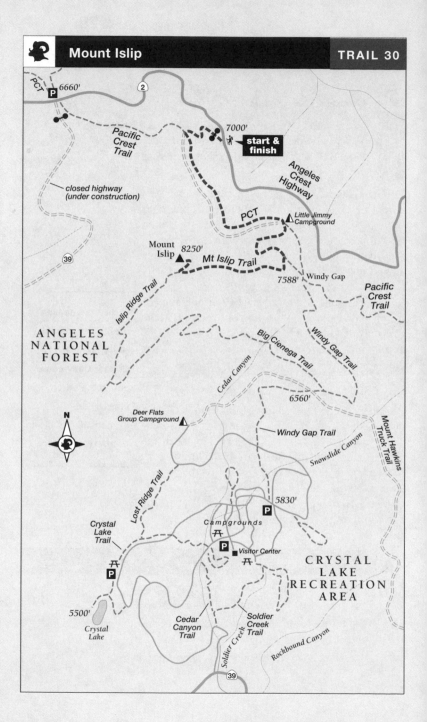

PCT

P 6660'

2

Pacific
Crest
Trail

closed highway
(under construction)

39

7000'

start &
finish

Angeles
Crest
Highway

Little Jimmy
Campground

PCT

Mount
Islip

8250'

Mt Islip Trail

7588'

Windy Gap

Pacific
Crest
Trail

Islip Ridge Trail

ANGELES
NATIONAL
FOREST

Cedar Canyon

Big Cienega Trail

Windy Gap Trail

6560'

N

Deer Flats
Group Campground

Windy Gap Trail

Snowslide Canyon

Mount Hawkins Truck Trail

Lost Ridge Trail

5830'

P

Campgrounds

P

Crystal
Lake
Trail

Visitor Center

P

CRYSTAL
LAKE
RECREATION
AREA

5500'

Crystal
Lake

Cedar
Canyon
Trail

Soldier
Creek
Trail

Soldier Creek

Rockbound Canyon

39

Mount Islip

Mount Islip, a rounded summit easily accessible from Angeles Crest Highway, offers a panoramic view north over the Mojave Desert and south over the metropolis. The gradually ascending northern route to the top takes you through aromatic pine and fir forest most of the way. Secluded Little Jimmy Campground, 1.5 miles up the slope, offers an intermediate destination for light hiking or for parents with smaller kids.

Best Time

The trails at this elevation are typically snow-free May through November. Angeles Crest Highway may be closed during significant portions of the winter and early spring due to heavy snowfall or landslide damage.

Finding the Trail

From Interstate 210 in La Cañada, drive 41 miles on Angeles Crest Highway to a gated fire road on the south side of the road. This starting point is at mile 65.5 according to the roadside mileage markers. A National Forest Adventure Pass is required for parking here.

Trail Description

Walk up the pine-cone-strewn road▶1 to where the **Pacific Crest Trail** crosses it,▶2 0.5 mile up and 350 feet higher. Both the road and the PCT go south and east to Little **Jimmy Campground**, but the trail

TRAIL USE
Hike, Run
LENGTH
5.6 miles, 3 hours
ELEVATION GAIN/LOSS
1250'/1250'
DIFFICULTY
– 1 **2** 3 4 5 +
TRAIL TYPE
Out & Back
SURFACE TYPE
Dirt

FEATURES
Permit Required
Dogs Allowed
Mountain
Summit
Secluded
Great Views
Camping
Moonlight Hiking

is nicer to follow on foot. The campground▶3 nestles comfortably in a little flat shaded by statuesque pines. Tables and stoves make this a convenient spot for a picnic or an overnight layover. Down the trail contouring south toward Windy Gap (below the trail .25 mile away) you might be able to find year-round Little Jimmy Spring.

 Camping

Little Jimmy Campground honors early-20th-century newspaper cartoonist Jimmy Swinnerton, the creator of the *Little Jimmy* comic strip. Swinnerton spent much of the summer of 1909 at this pleasant site, which was remote and isolated at that time.

Your route from the campground, however, takes off uphill on a curvy course that soon gains Mount Islip's east shoulder. (Stay right where a trail slants left and descends to meet the PCT).▶4 You ascend along Islip's airy flank, swing around two switchbacks just below the summit, and arrive at the top.▶5

Great Views

On the summit you'll discover the shell of an old stone cabin, and footings of a fire lookout tower that stood on Islip from 1927 until 1937. In 1937, the lookout was moved to a better site to the southeast—South Mount Hawkins. The South Mount Hawkins lookout structure was completely destroyed in the 2002 Curve Fire, but plans are afoot to rebuild it.

When you've had your fill of the rarefied air and exhilarating view, return to Angeles Crest Highway on the same route.

Mountain Biking

OPTIONS

Mountain bikers may follow the 1.5-mile long dirt road to Little Jimmy Campground, but bikes are not allowed on any section of the Pacific Crest Trail. A southern, more difficult route to Mount Islip originates at the Crystal Lake Recreation Area, off Highway 39 north of Azusa. Much of the Crystal Lake basin was severely burned in the 2002 fire, and it will be a while before the area fully recovers.

MILESTONES

▶1   0.0 Walk up fire road

▶2   0.5 Pacific Crest Trail crosses road; follow PCT south (uphill)

▶3   1.6 Arrive at Little Jimmy Campground; continue on upslope trail toward Mount Islip

▶4   2.0 Trail junction; stay right and continue climbing

▶5   2.8 Reach Mount Islip summit; return by the same route

Snow plant *grows around the 7000-foot elevation. Its bright red stalks push up from the soil soon after the snow melts.*

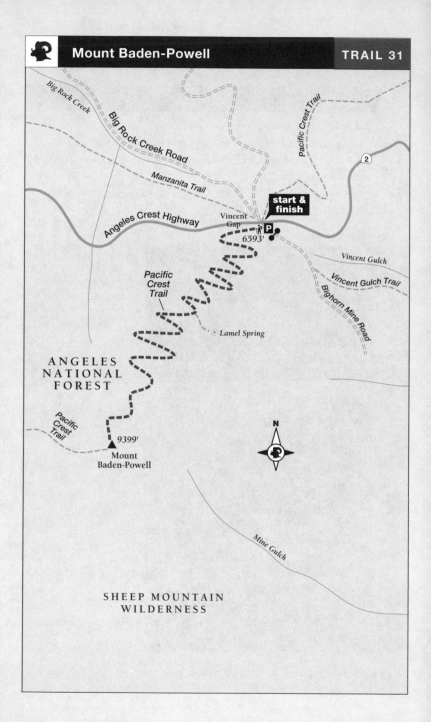

Big Rock Creek

Big Rock Creek Road

Pacific Crest Trail

②

Manzanita Trail

Angeles Crest Highway

Vincent Gap

start & finish

6593'

Ⓟ

Vincent Gulch

Vincent Gulch Trail

Bighorn Mine Road

Pacific Crest Trail

Lamel Spring

ANGELES NATIONAL FOREST

Pacific Crest Trail

9399'

▲

Mount Baden-Powell

N

Mine Gulch

SHEEP MOUNTAIN WILDERNESS

Mount Baden-Powell

Named in honor of Lord Baden-Powell, the British Army officer who started the Boy Scout movement in 1907, Mount Baden-Powell (elevation 9399 feet) stands higher than any other mountain in the San Gabriels—except the Mount San Antonio (Old Baldy) complex to the east. Thousands of hikers troop to Baden-Powell's summit yearly, and so should you! The trek is an excellent warm-up for the somewhat more difficult hike to the summit of San Jacinto Peak (see Trail 48, p. 255), and the much more difficult trip to the top of San Gorgonio Mountain (see Trail 47, p. 249).

Best Time

The uppermost part of this high-elevation, north-slope trail may be clogged with snow as late as May. Snowfall usually resumes in November or December. The access road to the trailhead, Angeles Crest Highway, may be closed during winter and early spring due to heavy snows or landslide damage.

Finding the Trail

From Interstate 210 in La Cañada, drive 50 miles east on Angeles Crest Highway to the Vincent Gap parking area (mile 74.8 according to the roadside mile markers. Alternately, you can approach Vincent Gap by way of Interstate 15, Highway 138, and Highway 2 (Angeles Crest Highway) through Wrightwood. Vincent Gap is 10 miles west of Wrightwood via Angeles Crest Highway. This eastern approach is decidedly faster for those coming from the eastern San Gabriel Valley, Orange County, and the Inland

TRAIL USE
Hike, Run
LENGTH
7.6 miles, 4.5 hours
ELEVATION GAIN/LOSS
2800'/2800'
DIFFICULTY
– 1 2 **3** 4 5 +
TRAIL TYPE
Out & Back
SURFACE TYPE
Dirt

FEATURES
Permit Required
Dogs Allowed
Mountain
Summit
Wildlife
Great Views
Photo Opportunity
Camping
Moonlight Hiking

Limber pines are limber—or at least their twigs are. But don't bend excessively the branches of these rare trees to prove that point.

Empire region. A **National Forest Adventure Pass** is required to park at Vincent Gap.

Trail Description

From Vincent Gap, the trail (a segment of the Pacific Crest Trail) ►1 begins a no-nonsense ascent of Baden-Powell's northeast flank. Along the way you'll reverse course 40 times on switchback corners, following trail segments of various lengths between the corners. At about 1.5 miles, a minor side trail at one of the switchback corners►2 leads about 200 yards east to a dribbling pipe at **Lamel Spring**. Otherwise, navigation is simple—just keep going up. Snow cover can make staying on the trail problematical.

The entire ascent could serve as a lengthy natural-history lesson about the relationship between flora and elevation. You begin amid oaks and Jeffrey pines, pass through a zone rich in white firs, and finally—near the top—enter a sparse forest of lodgepole and rare (for Southern California, anyway) limber pines. How do you tell the difference between lodgepole and limber? Lodgepole pine needles come in bundles of two each, while limber pines have needles in bundles of five.

▲ **Summit**

Baden-Powell's summit area►3 includes an impressive **Boy Scout monument**, and several starkly photogenic, weatherbeaten lodgepole and limber pine trees. Sightings of Nelson bighorn sheep are not uncommon on the upper slopes of Baden-Powell—so be prepared with your camera to zoom from a wide-angle perspective of a statuesque tree to a long shot of bighorn.

📷 **Photo Opportunity**

Baden-Powell's summit is the last major milestone on the 52-mile trek from Chantry Flat to Vincent Gap, known as the Silver Moccasin Trail (which in this part of the range coincides with the Pacific Crest Trail). The five-day-long Silver Moccasin backpack is a rite of passage for L.A.-area Scouts.

MILESTONES

▶1   0.0 Follow Pacific Crest Trail up the mountain slope
▶2   1.5 Side trail goes left to Lamel Spring
▶3   3.8 Reach summit of Mount Baden-Powell; return by same route

Lodgepole pine snag
atop Mt. Baden-Powell

Backpacking

OPTIONS

For backpackers, no-trace wilderness campsites can be established
near Baden-Powell's summit, or on the ridgeline to the south.
Permits are not required, though it is wise to contact Angeles
National Forest first.

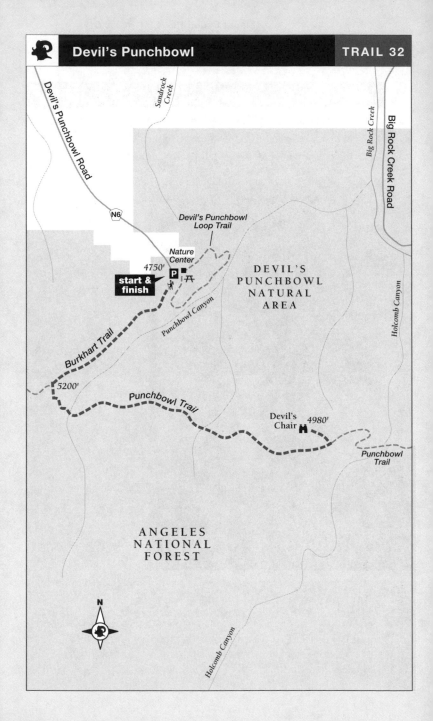

Devil's Punchbowl Road

Sandrock Creek

Big Rock Creek

Big Rock Creek Road

N6

Devil's Punchbowl
Loop Trail

Nature
Center

4750'

**start &
finish**

DEVIL'S
PUNCHBOWL
NATURAL
AREA

Punchbowl Canyon

Holcomb Canyon

Burkhart Trail

5200'

Punchbowl Trail

Devil's
Chair 4980'

Punchbowl
Trail

ANGELES
NATIONAL
FOREST

N

Holcomb Canyon

Devil's Punchbowl

Tens of millions of years in the making, Devil's Punchbowl is without a doubt L.A. County's most spectacular geological showplace. This trail takes you to the viewpoint called the Devil's Chair, where you gaze upon what looks like frozen chaos—a vast assemblage of sandstone chunks and slabs tipped at odd angles, bent, seemingly pulled apart here, compressed there. This is really not so surprising when you realize that the Punchbowl is underlain by two faults: the Punchbowl Fault and the mighty San Andreas Fault.

Best Time

There are two best seasons for the Punchbowl trek: September through November, and March through May. Winter is fine as long as little or no snow lies on the ground. Summer days are almost always uncomfortably warm.

Finding the Trail

Exit the Antelope Valley Freeway (Highway 14) at Pearblossom Highway, and follow it east through the town of Littlerock to Pearblossom. At Pearblossom, turn right on Longview Road (County N6) and follow signs for **Devil's Punchbowl Natural Area**, 7 miles away. The park is open daily from sunrise to sunset, no admission charge. There's free parking at the visitor center (open daily from 9 A.M. to 4 P.M.). If snow is on the ground, ask at the visitor center if the Punchbowl Trail route is safe. The visitor center's telephone is (661) 944-2743.

TRAIL USE
Hike, Run
LENGTH
6.2 miles, 3 hours
ELEVATION GAIN/LOSS
1200'/1200'
DIFFICULTY
– 1 2 **3** 4 5 +
TRAIL TYPE
Out & Back
SURFACE TYPE
Dirt

FEATURES
Dogs Allowed
Mountain
Wildflowers
Birds
Wildlife
Great View
Photo Opportunity
Geologic Interest

In late spring, the
blooming yuccas
alongside the trail
look as if they are
sprouting shimmering
white exclamation
points.

Trail Description

From the south side of the visitor center parking lot, find and follow the signed **Burkhart Trail**▶1 as it climbs southwest along the rim of the Punchbowl, which lies on the left. You're actually following the upper edge of a downward sloping terrace—part of an alluvial fan left high and dry when the nearby creek draining into the Punchbowl began carving a new course northeast. The sedimentary formations inside the Punchbowl have been pushed upward and crumpled downward, as well as transported horizontally. Erosion has put the final touches on the scene, roughing out the bowl-shaped gorge and carving, in many unique ways, the rocks exposed at the surface.

You join an old road at 0.5 mile, pass a small reservoir at 0.7 mile, and arrive at a trail junction at 0.8 mile.▶2 Here, in a Coulter-pine grove, bear left on the **Punchbowl Trail** (a part of the longer High Desert National Recreation Trail) leading east. This delightful, contouring path takes you around several shady ravines, all draining into the Punchbowl. After some sharply descending switchbacks, you

 Photo Opportunity

reach a trail junction▶3 (3.0 miles) from where a 0.1-mile spur travels over a narrow, rock-ribbed ridge to the high perch known as Devil's Chair.▶4 Protective fencing furnishes some psychological comfort for the nervous-making traverse.

OPTIONS

Devil's Punchbowl

A shorter, tamer trek—especially good for small children—is the mile-long **Devil's Punchbowl Loop Trail**, which begins at the visitor center. It meanders among jumbo-sized sandstone formations and dips to cross a seasonal creek.

A slightly shorter, eastern route to Devil's Chair starts at South Fork Campground, in the Angeles National Forest. The dirt access road into the campground may be seasonally closed.

Devil's Punchbowl *with a dusting of snow*

On clear early mornings or late afternoons, the sunlight slanting sideways across the sandstone formations inside the Punchbowl produces an otherworldly scene. When you've had your fill of this visual bonanza, turn around and return the same way you came.

Geologic Interest

The vegetation along the Punchbowl Trail is an interesting blend between the pine forests of the higher San Gabriels and the pinyon-juniper woodland and chaparral scrub of the uppermost Mojave Desert rim.

🚶 MILESTONES

▶1 0.0 Follow Burkhart Trail uphill
▶2 0.8 Trail junction; go left on Punchbowl Trail
▶3 3.0 Turn left on spur trail to Devil's Chair
▶4 3.1 Arrive at Devil's Chair overlook; return by same route

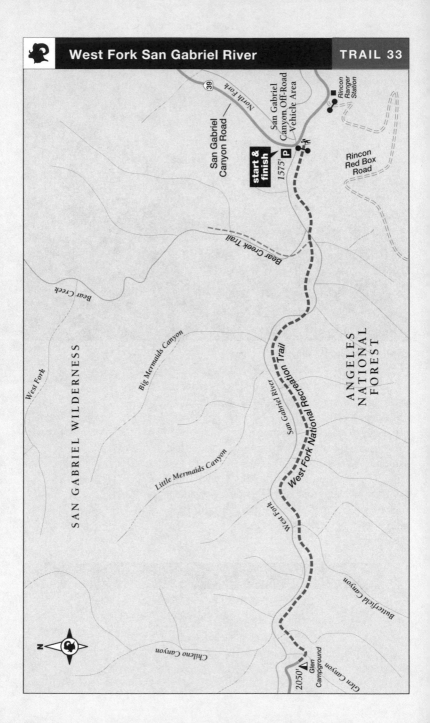

(39)

North Fork

San Gabriel
Canyon Off-Road
Vehicle Area

Rincon
Ranger
Station

San Gabriel Canyon Road

start &
finish

1575'

P

Rincon
Red Box
Road

Bear Creek Trail

Bear Creek

San Gabriel River

Big Mermaids Canyon

ANGELES
NATIONAL
FOREST

West Fork

SAN GABRIEL WILDERNESS

West Fork National Recreation Trail

Little Mermaids Canyon

West Fork

Butterfield Canyon

N

Chileno Canyon

Glen Canyon

2050'

Glen
Campground

West Fork San Gabriel River

The West Fork National Recreation Trail is by far the most perfect, easy bicycling route in the L.A. region. This hard-surfaced service road, closed to all but administrative motor traffic, follows for several miles the beautiful West Fork of the San Gabriel River. Shaded by riparian vegetation, flanked by sometimes sheer rock walls, and accompanied always by the murmur of the river, cyclists feel as if they're pedaling through a wonderland. The return ride is even better—an occasional turn or two of the crank is all that's needed to keep that two-wheeled machine coasting. The West Fork trail also serves as a good, long workout for runners and long-distance hikers—though hikers may find the going a little monotonous after the first couple of hours.

Best Time

Although the West Fork Trail is pleasant virtually any time of year, the scenery is particularly stunning in the spring, when the stream is running well and wildflowers are blooming. Summer may bring the annoyance of gnats and other flying insects. Afternoon smog drifting up into the mountains from the San Gabriel Valley can spoil the aesthetic experience, as well as affect your breathing. It's usually best to be here in the morning.

Finding the Trail

From the community of Azusa, just north of Interstate 210, follow **Highway 39** north for 12 miles to a parking area just beyond (north of) the West Fork

TRAIL USE
Hike, Run, Bike
LENGTH
12.6 miles, 5 hours
ELEVATION GAIN/LOSS
500'/500'
DIFFICULTY
− 1 2 **3** 4 5 +
TRAIL TYPE
Out & Back
SURFACE TYPE
Asphalt

FEATURES
Permit Required
Dogs Allowed
Child Friendly
Canyon
Streams
Waterfall
Wildflowers
Birds
Wildlife
Cool & Shady
Photo Opportunity
Camping
Moonlight Hiking

West Fork National Recreation Trail

The West Fork San Gabriel River is one of the few remaining freshwater aquatic habitats in Southern California that support a wide variety of rare native fish.

San Gabriel River bridge. (You reach this bridge after passing the Rincon Ranger Station and the San Gabriel Canyon off-road-vehicle area.) Parking here requires a National Forest Adventure Pass.

Trail Description

From the south end of the bridge, walk or wheel your bike around a vehicle gate onto the **West Fork National Recreation Trail.▶1** This paved service road follows the gentle twists and turns of the West Fork to the top of Cogswell Dam, 7.5 miles away, but another gate just short of that destination has blocked all access to the dam site since the events of September 11, 2001. There is no scheduled date for restoring public access to the dam.

Once you get past the first graffiti-scarred mile or so, the remainder of the West Fork route is exceedingly pleasant. Fishing is popular on the initial stretch to as far as the second bridge. Beyond that, the rules permit catch-and-release fishing only.

After 1 mile you'll come to the mouth of **Bear Creek canyon▶2** on the right (north) side. A sketchy, unmaintained trail—more of a boulder-hopping route actually—works its way several miles up this canyon. On the left side of the West Fork canyon, following heavy rains, you may get to enjoy several small cascades of water tumbling down various side ravines.

After 6.3 miles of riding, and nearly 500 feet of elevation gain, you reach **Glen Campground▶3** (hike-in or bike-in only; first-come, first served). This lies at the end of the gradually ascending stretch of the service road, and is the logical place for taking an extended rest or having lunch. Turn back from this point and enjoy the downhill return route.

Humans aren't the only fishers on the West Fork. Keep an eye out for great blue herons in the shallows of the river.

 Wildlife

🚶	**MILESTONES**
▶1	0.0 Take the West Fork Trail (gated, paved road) west
▶2	1.0 Pass mouth of Bear Creek canyon on the right
▶3	6.3 Arrive at Glen Campground, the turnround point

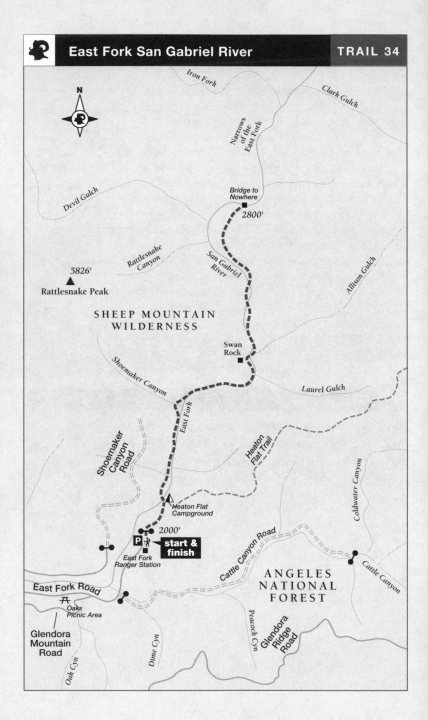

Iron Fork

Clark Gulch

Narrows
of the
East Fork

Devil Gulch

Bridge to
Nowhere

2800'

Rattlesnake
Canyon

San Gabriel
River

Allison Gulch

5826'
▲
Rattlesnake Peak

SHEEP MOUNTAIN
WILDERNESS

Swan
Rock

Shoemaker Canyon

Laurel Gulch

East Fork

Shoemaker
Canyon
Road

Heaton
Flat Trail

Coldwater Canyon

Heaton Flat
Campground

2000'

P

start &
finish

East Fork
Ranger Station

Cattle Canyon Road

Cattle Canyon

ANGELES
NATIONAL
FOREST

East Fork Road

Oaks
Picnic Area

Peacock Cyn

Glendora
Ridge
Road

Glendora
Mountain
Road

Oak Cyn

Dime Cyn

East Fork San Gabriel River

Born of snow-fed rivulets, the many tributaries of the East Fork of the San Gabriel River gather together to form one of the liveliest mountain streams in the San Gabriel Mountains. Along a section called "The Narrows," the East Fork squeezes through the deepest gorge in Southern California. At the lower portal of this gorge, miles from any existing roadway, stands the curious "Bridge to Nowhere," a relic of an attempt in the 1930s to establish a highway link between the San Gabriel Valley and Wrightwood. A catastrophic flood in 1938 demolished most of the road-to-be, leaving the bridge stranded upstream. Today, a visit to the Bridge to Nowhere is practically obligatory for L.A.-area hikers.

TRAIL USE
Hike, Run
LENGTH
9.6 miles, 5 hours
ELEVATION GAIN/LOSS
1000'/1000'
DIFFICULTY
– 1 2 **3** 4 5 +
TRAIL TYPE
Out & Back
SURFACE TYPE
Dirt

FEATURES
Permit Required
Dogs Allowed
Canyon
Stream
Wildflowers
Birds
Wildlife
Camping
Historic

Best Time

The trick is to do this hike on a relatively cool day— with enough flowing water in the river to make things interesting but not scary at the several places where you must wade across. This time frame would most likely be January through April in a year without much rain. In years of heavy rain, you might need to wait until summer for safe conditions. If you go during a hot summer day, keep yourself cool by splashing river water on yourself at every stream crossing. Contact Angeles National Forest, (626) 574-5200, for information and advice.

Finding the Trail

From the community of Azusa, just north of Interstate 210, drive north on the San Gabriel Canyon

Bridge to Nowhere

Road, Highway 39, for 11 miles to East Fork Road, on the right. Continue up **East Fork Road** 6 miles to its terminus near the East Fork ranger station. Park here, and don't forget to display a National Forest Adventure Pass on your car. Also don't forget to fill out a wilderness permit at the self-issuing register before you start your hike or run.

Further Exploring

OPTIONS

From the north abutment of the **Bridge to Nowhere**, a narrow trail contours above the stream, then drops into the lower part of The Narrows. For backpackers and adventurous hikers, that's were the real fun begins—assuming the water isn't flowing too swiftly. It's possible to press onward for several miles using a sketchy trail along the East Fork banks, visiting side canyons that harbor small waterfalls in their middle and upper extremities.

Trail Description

Follow the gated service road upstream from the East Fork trailhead,►1 high along the right bank, to Heaton Flat Campground,►2 0.5 mile. Beyond Heaton Flat the road ends, but a well-traveled trail continues up the flood plain. You might as well resign yourself to getting your shoes or boots wet; there are several ankle- or calf-deep river crossings ahead.

At 2.5 miles, you pass **Swan Rock,**►3 a cliff-exposure of metamorphic rock branded with the light-colored imprint of a swan. You can see it best under cloudy or open-shade lighting conditions. You're now entering **Sheep Mountain Wilderness**.

At 3.5 miles, the trail swings abruptly right►4 and climbs about 60 feet to meet a remnant of the never-completed highway. The old road bed carves its way along the east canyon wall, high above what is now a wide, boulder-filled flood plain laced with the meandering, alder-lined stream. The **Bridge to Nowhere**►5 appears at 4.8 miles, just as the canyon walls start to pinch in. The bridge appears remarkably intact after many decades of neglect, except for its crumbling concrete railings.

The bridge and the area just south of it lie within an island of posted private property. You're allowed passage across the bridge, but please don't stray from the road or the bridge when you're inside the posted area.

The Narrows of the East Fork is the low point in Southern California's deepest gorge. From the bottom to top, the "walls" of the gorge soar as high as 5200 feet on the east side, and 4000 feet on the west side.

 Wildflowers

⚐	MILESTONES	
►1	0.0	Follow service road toward Heaton Flat
►2	0.5	Pass through Heaton Flat Campground; continue upsteam in flood plain
►3	2.5	Pass Swan Rock on left (west) side of canyon
►4	3.5	Trail climbs to follow a remnant of pavement
►5	4.8	Arrive at Bridge to Nowhere; then return by same route

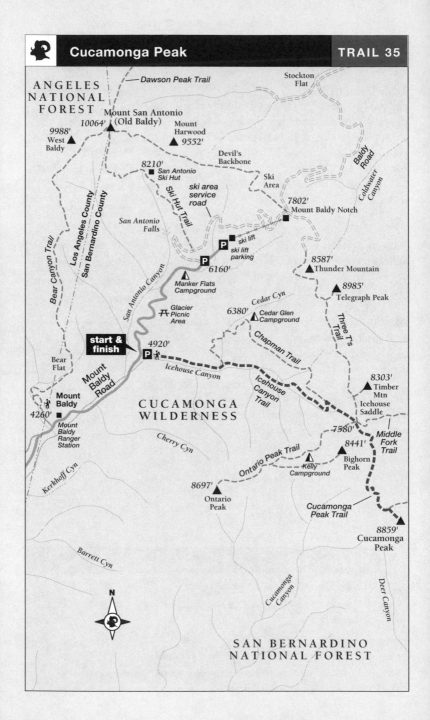

ANGELES
NATIONAL
FOREST

Dawson Peak Trail

Stockton
Flat

Mount San Antonio
(Old Baldy)

10064'

9988'
West
Baldy

Mount
Harwood
9552'

8210'
San Antonio
Ski Hut

Devil's
Backbone

Baldy
Road

Ski
Area

Coldwater
Canyon

7802'
Mount Baldy Notch

ski area
service
road

Ski Hut Trail

San Antonio
Falls

San Antonio Canyon

Bear Canyon Trail

Los Angeles County
San Bernardino County

ski lift

ski lift
parking

6160'

Manker Flats
Campground

8587'
Thunder Mountain

8985'
Telegraph Peak

Glacier
Picnic
Area

Cedar Cyn

6380'

Cedar Glen
Campground

Three T's Trail

**start &
finish**

4920'

Chapman Trail

Icehouse Canyon

Bear
Flat

Mount Baldy Road

Icehouse
Canyon
Trail

8303'
Timber
Mtn

Icehouse
Saddle

Mount
Baldy

4260'

Mount
Baldy
Ranger
Station

CUCAMONGA
WILDERNESS

Cherry Cyn

Kerkhoff Cyn

Ontario Peak Trail

7580'

8441'

Kelly
Campground

Bighorn
Peak

*Middle
Fork
Trail*

8697'

Ontario
Peak

*Cucamonga
Peak Trail*

Cucamonga Canyon

Deer Canyon

8859'
Cucamonga
Peak

Barrett Cyn

N

SAN BERNARDINO
NATIONAL FOREST

Cucamonga Peak

Cucamonga Peak's south and east slopes feature some of the most dramatic relief in the San Gabriel range. At 8859 feet, the peak stands sentinel-like, only 4 miles from the edge of the broad inland valley region known as the Inland Empire. Stupendous views are the best reward for summiting (in clear-air conditions, at any rate)—yet so much beautiful high country can be seen along the way that reaching the top is just icing on the cake. The upper two-thirds of the trail lies within Cucamonga Wilderness, which requires a wilderness permit for day and overnight use. Obtain one in advance by visiting the Mount Baldy ranger station or visitor center in the village of Mount Baldy—or contact Angeles National Forest at (626) 574-5200.

Best Time

Summer though fall are the best seasons. Summer thundershowers occasionally develop over this part of the range, but with an early enough start you can be finished with your hike or run before any big cumulonimbus clouds brew up. Another hazard is snow and ice. The north slope of Cucamonga Peak retains snow into May. Be sure to discuss with a ranger the possible hazards of snow and ice if it's early or late in the season.

Finding the Trail

Exit the 210 Freeway at Mills Avenue in Claremont, and follow Mills north toward the mountains. After about a mile Mills becomes Mount Baldy Road. An

TRAIL USE
Hike, Run
LENGTH
12.0 miles, 7 hours
ELEVATION GAIN/LOSS
4300'/4300'
DIFFICULTY
– 1 2 3 **4** 5 +
TRAIL TYPE
Out & Back
SURFACE TYPE
Dirt

FEATURES
Permit Required
Dogs Allowed
Canyon
Mountain
Summit
Streams
Waterfall
Wildflowers
Cool & Shady
Great Views
Photo Opportunity
Camping
Historic
Steep

8-mile climb up through San Antonio Canyon on **Mount Baldy Road** takes you to the village of Mount Baldy. Continue 1.5 miles past the village to a short **spur road** on the right, signed "No Outlet." Park at the end of that spur, and don't forget to post a National Forest Adventure Pass on your car.

Trail Description

Walk up the **Icehouse Canyon Trail►1** following a beautiful, alder-shaded stream. If you're trying to run the route, take it easy at the beginning—get warmed up first and watch your footing on the initially rocky trail.

The first couple of miles along Icehouse Canyon are a fitting introduction to a phase of Southern California scenery not familiar to a lot of visitors and newcomers. Huge bigcone Douglas-fir, incense cedar, and live oak trees cluster on the banks of the stream, which dances over boulder and fallen log. Moisture-loving, flowering plants like columbine sway in the breeze.

 Historic

Whether ice was once quarried in this canyon or in another nearby, Icehouse Canyon's name is apt enough: cold-air drainage produces refrigeratorlike temperatures on many a summer morning, and deep-freeze temperatures in winter.

🚶	MILESTONES	
►1	0.0	Take the Icehouse Canyon Trail
►2	1.0	Chapman Trail intersects on the left; keep straight
►3	2.4	Trail starts ascending canyon slope to the left
►4	2.9	Chapman Trail (upper intersection) is on the left; stay right
►5	3.5	Reach Icehouse Saddle; follow trail to Cucamonga Peak
►6	4.4	Reach saddle between Bighorn and Cucamonga peaks
►7	5.8	Take faint side path on the right directly to Cucamonga summit
►8	6.0	Arrive at Cucamonga Peak summit; return by the same route

Camping

Backpackers can use Cedar **Glen Trail Camp** as an overnight staging area, and then day hike to Cucamonga Peak on the following morning. It is also possible to pitch a tent in other areas of the Cucamonga Wilderness.

The Chapman Trail, leading toward Cedar Glen Trail Camp, intersects on the left▶2 at 1.0 mile. At **Columbine Spring**, 2.4 miles,▶3 the trail starts switchbacking up the canyon's north wall. After passing the upper intersection of the Chapman Trail▶4 at 2.9 miles, you continue to pine-shaded **Icehouse Saddle**,▶5 3.5 miles, where trails converge from many directions. The trail to Cucamonga's summit contours southeast, descends moderately, and climbs to a 7654-foot saddle (4.4 miles) between **Bighorn** and **Cucamonga** peaks.▶6 Thereafter, it switchbacks up a steep slope dotted with lodgepole pines and white firs.

At 5.8 miles, the trail crosses a shady draw 200 feet below and northwest of the Cucamonga summit.▶7 A signed but indistinct side path goes straight up to the summit,▶8 6.0 miles from your starting point in Icehouse Canyon. Enjoy the view— then get psyched up for the trip back down the mountain. The 4000-foot loss of elevation may seem like a piece of cake, but your fatigued body may tell you otherwise during your descent.

 ▲ Summit

Further Exploring

From Icehouse Saddle, the **Three T's Trail** heads north past three peaks with "T" initials, and drops into Mount Baldy Notch, where it's possible to ride a ski lift down to the upper end of Mount Baldy Road. This link makes possible a long looping route—a good one for runners especially—that could take you back the Icehouse Canyon trailhead.

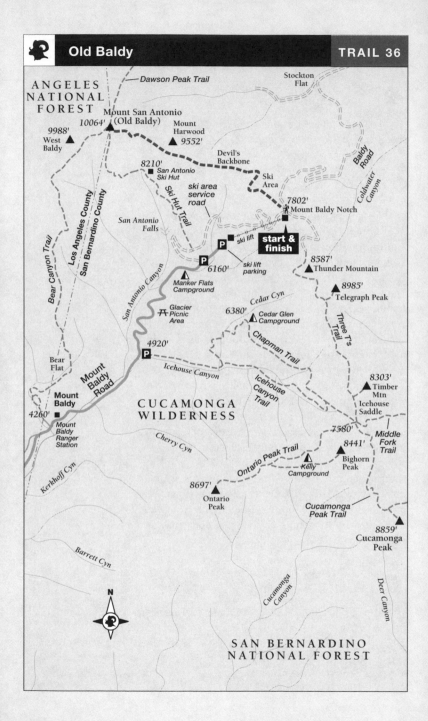

ANGELES
NATIONAL
FOREST

Dawson Peak Trail

Stockton
Flat

Mount San Antonio
(Old Baldy)
10064'

9988'
West
Baldy

Mount
Harwood
9552'

Devil's
Backbone

8210'
San Antonio
Ski Hut

ski area
service
road

Ski
Area

Baldy
Road

Coldwater
Canyon

7802'
Mount Baldy Notch

Ski Hut Trail

San Antonio
Falls

ski lift

start &
finish

P

P

6160'

ski lift
parking

8587'
Thunder Mountain

Los Angeles County
San Bernardino County

Bear Canyon Trail

Manker Flats
Campground

Cedar Cyn

8985'
Telegraph Peak

San Antonio Canyon

Glacier
Picnic
Area

6380'

Cedar Glen
Campground

Chapman Trail

Three T's Trail

4920'
P

Icehouse Canyon

Bear
Flat

Mount Baldy Road

8303'
Timber
Mtn
Icehouse
Saddle

Mount Baldy

Icehouse Canyon Trail

Middle
Fork
Trail

4260'

Mount
Baldy
Ranger
Station

CUCAMONGA
WILDERNESS

Cherry Cyn

7580'

8441'
Bighorn
Peak

Kerhkoff Cyn

Ontario Peak Trail

Kelly
Campground

8697'
Ontario
Peak

Cucamonga
Peak Trail

Barrett Cyn

8859'
Cucamonga
Peak

N

Cucamonga
Canyon

Deer Canyon

SAN BERNARDINO
NATIONAL FOREST

Old Baldy

No Southland hiker's repertoire of experiences is complete without at least one ascent of Mount San Antonio, or "Old Baldy." At 10,064 feet, Baldy's summit looms large over the eastern Los Angeles Basin, the Inland Empire communities of Riverside and San Bernardino, and the western Mojave Desert. The mountain can be seen as far north as the southern Sierra Nevada and as far south as the Mexican border adjoining San Diego County. Those facts indicate how magnificent the view from the top can be on a clear day. The east, or Devil's Backbone, approach described here is the least taxing of the several routes to the summit, but it's by no means a picnic. You start at 7800 feet, with virtually no altitude acclimatization, and climb expeditiously to over 10,000 feet in just over 3 miles.

Best Time

From the time of melting snows in May or June until the first major winter storm in November or December, the Devil's Backbone route to Old Baldy's summit is good for both hiking and strenuous running. Summer thunderstorms may brew up over the mountain July through early September; an early start is advised during periods when that monsoon-type of weather pattern persists.

Finding the Trail

By mechanical means (a car) you can get to the upper terminus of Mount Baldy Road in less than half an hour from the valley flatlands below (see

TRAIL USE
Hike, Run
LENGTH
6.4 miles, 3.5 hours
ELEVATION GAIN/LOSS
2300'/2300'
DIFFICULTY
− 1 2 **3** 4 5 +
TRAIL TYPE
Out & Back
SURFACE TYPE
Dirt

FEATURES
Dogs Allowed
Mountain
Summit
Birds
Wildlife
Great Views
Photo Opportunity
Camping
Steep

> On days of crystalline clarity, the Old Baldy panorama includes 90 degrees of ocean horizon, a 120-degree slice of the tawny desert floor, and the far-off ramparts of the southern Sierra Nevada and Panamint ranges, as far as 160 miles away.

Great Views

Trail 35, p. 185, for details of how to head this way). By further mechanical means, the Mount Baldy ski lift, you rise to **Mount Baldy Notch** (elevation 7800 feet), where you begin hiking. Although the ski lift caters mostly to skiers (seven days a week during the winter season), it remains open during the summer season on weekends (9:00 A.M. to 4:45 P.M.) for the benefit of sightseers and hikers. If it's a weekday, or you don't like being dangled over an abyss, you can always walk up the ski-lift maintenance road, starting from **Manker Flats**. That option adds 3.6 miles and an elevation change of about 1600 feet both on the way up and on the way down.

Trail Description

From Mount Baldy Notch, technically the spot about 200 yards northeast of the top of the main ski lift, take the maintenance road▶1 to the northwest, which climbs moderately, then more steeply through groves of Jeffrey pine and incense cedar. After a couple of bends, you come to the road's end▶2 (1.3 miles) and the beginning of the narrow trail along the **Devil's Backbone** ridge.

The stretch ahead, once a hair-raiser, lost most of its terror when the Civilian Conservation Corps constructed a wider and safer trail, complete with guard rails, in 1935-36. The guard rails are gone now, but there's plenty of room to maneuver, unless there are problems with strong winds and/or ice. Devil's Backbone offers grand vistas of both the Lytle Creek drainage on the north and east and San Antonio Canyon on the south.

The backbone section ends at about 2.0 miles, as you start traversing the broad south flank of Mount Harwood. Scattered lodgepole pines now predominate. At 2.6 miles you arrive at the saddle between Harwood and Old Baldy,▶3 where backpackers sometimes set up camp (no water, no facilities here). Continue climbing up the rocky ridge to the west, past stunted, wind-battered conifers barely clinging to survival in the face of yearly onslaughts by cold winter winds. You reach the summit▶4 after a total of 3.2 miles.

 Summit

On the rocky summit, barren of trees, you'll find a rock-walled enclosure and a register book which, on a fair-weather weekend, fills up with the names of hundreds of hikers. Most days you can easily make out the other two members of the triad of Southern California giants—**San Gorgonio Mountain** and **San Jacinto Peak**—about 50 miles east and southeast, respectively.

A lodge at the top of the ski lift offers food and beverages—your reward when you return.

MILESTONES

▶1   0.0   Follow maintenance road uphill (northwest) from top of ski lift

▶2   1.3   Maintenance road ends, and narrow Devil's Backbone Trail begins

▶3   2.6   Arrive at saddle between Mt. Harwood and Old Baldy; trail turns sharply uphill ahead

▶4   3.2   Arrive at Old Baldy summit; return by the same route

Other Routes to Old Baldy

OPTIONS

A lesser traveled, more difficult way to approach Old Baldy's summit includes the Ski Hut Trail, which takes off from the ski-lift service road a short distance above San Antonio Falls. This steep route gains 3900 feet in just 4.2 miles. For the truly masochistic hiker or runner, there's the Bear Canyon Trail, which starts in Mount Baldy village and climbs 5800 feet in 6.4 miles—practically straight up the mountain's south ridge.

Orange County

Orange County

The tide of Orange County's suburban sprawl is pressing against some firm boundaries. The rugged spines and canyons of the Santa Ana Mountains rise to the east, with Cleveland National Forest claiming most of them. Tens of thousands of acres of former ranching and grazing land from the south coast range of hills to the Santa Anas are gradually being deeded to the county by private land interests in exchange for development rights elsewhere. As a result, the east and south fringes of the Orange County are beginning to boast a rich assortment of spacious hike- and bike-friendly parks and open-space preserves.

This chapter selects the best outdoor experiences Orange County has to offer. It also includes a trail in the superb Santa Rosa Plateau Ecological Reserve, which lies in the nearby southwestern corner of Riverside County.

Permits and Maps

The Cleveland National Forest recreation map, available from the forest service and certain outdoor retailers, shows roads, trails, and public-private property boundaries throughout Orange County. For driving purposes, the Automobile Club of Southern California's *Los Angeles and Orange Counties and Vicinity* map is highly recommended.

Free trail-map leaflets are generally available at the parks and trailheads of the trails in this chapter, with the exception of the Main Divide route into the Santa Ana Mountains.

Since several different agencies manage parkland in the Orange County area, parking fees and policies can vary. See each trail description for the particulars.

Orange County

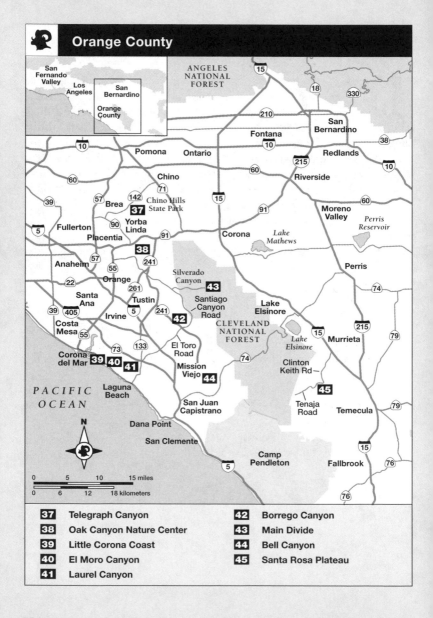

Orange County

San Fernando Valley

Los Angeles

San Bernardino

Orange County

ANGELES NATIONAL FOREST

Fontana

San Bernardino

Pomona

Ontario

Redlands

Chino

Riverside

Brea

Chino Hills State Park

Yorba Linda

Moreno Valley

Perris Reservoir

Fullerton

Placentia

Corona

Lake Mathews

Anaheim

Orange

Silverado Canyon

Perris

Santa Ana

Tustin

Santiago Canyon Road

Lake Elsinore

Irvine

Costa Mesa

Lake Elsinore

Murrieta

Corona del Mar

El Toro Road

CLEVELAND NATIONAL FOREST

PACIFIC OCEAN

Mission Viejo

Clinton Keith Rd

Laguna Beach

San Juan Capistrano

Tenaja Road

Temecula

Dana Point

San Clemente

Camp Pendleton

Fallbrook

N

0   5   10   15 miles

0   6   12   18 kilometers

37	Telegraph Canyon	42	Borrego Canyon
38	Oak Canyon Nature Center	43	Main Divide
39	Little Corona Coast	44	Bell Canyon
40	El Moro Canyon	45	Santa Rosa Plateau
41	Laurel Canyon		

Orange County Trails

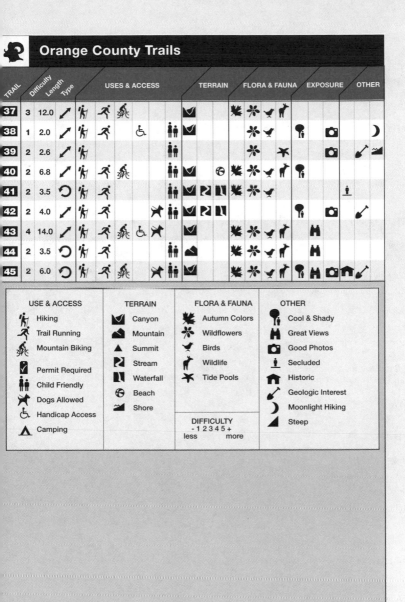

TRAIL	Difficulty	Length	Type	USES & ACCESS	TERRAIN	FLORA & FAUNA	EXPOSURE	OTHER
37	3	12.0						
38	1	2.0						
39	2	2.6						
40	2	6.8						
41	2	3.5						
42	2	4.0						
43	4	14.0						
44	2	3.5						
45	2	6.0						

USE & ACCESS
- Hiking
- Trail Running
- Mountain Biking
- Permit Required
- Child Friendly
- Dogs Allowed
- Handicap Access
- Camping

TERRAIN
- Canyon
- Mountain
- Summit
- Stream
- Waterfall
- Beach
- Shore

FLORA & FAUNA
- Autumn Colors
- Wildflowers
- Birds
- Wildlife
- Tide Pools

OTHER
- Cool & Shady
- Great Views
- Good Photos
- Secluded
- Historic
- Geologic Interest
- Moonlight Hiking
- Steep

DIFFICULTY
- 1 2 3 4 5 +
less   more

Orange County

Make your way up a densely shaded ravine in Orange County's Whiting Ranch Wilderness Park. Hike onward using a narrowing trail to visit the strangely weathered sandstone outcrops at Red Rock cliffs.

TRAIL 42

Hike, Run
4.0 miles, Out & Back
Difficulty: 1 **2** 3 4 5

Possibly tedious for hikers, but challenging and exhilarating for runners and mountain bikers, the long ascent via Maple Springs to the Main Divide of the Santa Ana Mountains rewards you with beautiful canyon scenery and superb views.

TRAIL 43

Hike, Run, Bike
14.0 miles, Out & Back
Difficulty: 1 2 3 **4** 5

Rise to a viewful ridgeline, then descend into the oak- and sycamore-lined Bell Canyon. This loop hike in Caspers Wilderness Park offers the best foothill scenery Orange County has to offer.

TRAIL 44

Hike, Run, Bike
3.5 miles, Loop
Difficulty: 1 **2** 3 4 5

Wind-rippled grasses, swaying California poppies, statuesque oak trees, trickling streams, and a 39-acre vernal pool—it's all there to see on a sunny spring day at the Santa Rosa Plateau Ecological Reserve.

TRAIL 45

Hike, Run, Bike
6.0 miles, Loop
Difficulty: 1 **2** 3 4 5

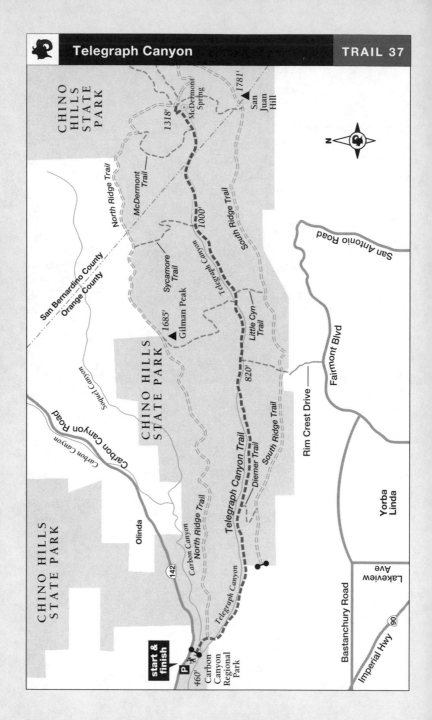

CHINO HILLS STATE PARK

1781'
San Juan Hill

McDermott Spring

1318'

McDermott Trail

North Ridge Trail

San Bernardino County
Orange County

1000'

South Ridge Trail

Sycamore Trail

Telegraph Canyon

1685'
Gilman Peak

Little Cyn Trail

820

Soquel Canyon

CHINO HILLS STATE PARK

San Antonio Road

Fairmont Blvd

Rim Crest Drive

Carbon Canyon Road

Carbon Canyon

South Ridge Trail

Telegraph Canyon Trail

Diemer Trail

Carbon Canyon
North Ridge Trail

Olinda

CHINO HILLS STATE PARK

142

Telegraph Canyon

start & finish
P
460'
Carbon Canyon Regional Park

Yorba Linda

Lakeview Ave

Bastanchury Road

Imperial Hwy
90

Telegraph Canyon

Whether you're a hiker, a runner, or a mountain biker, Telegraph Canyon in Chino Hills State Park offers a 6-mile spread of superb scenery for you to admire while you are working out. Try this trip sometime on a late-autumn afternoon, after the first rains of the season, when the sun's warm rays illuminate the gold and green sycamores, and the cool breeze has a tangy, woodsy aroma.

Best Time

Summer through early fall is normally very warm, though with an early start you can sometimes beat the heat. All other seasons are great. The park administration may temporarily close the trails in the state park if they get too muddy after a heavy winter or spring rain.

Finding the Trail

From the 57 Freeway in the suburb of Brea, exit at Lambert Road, and travel east. After 2 miles (at the intersection of Valencia Avenue) keep going straight on Carbon Canyon Road. Travel another mile to the entrance to **Carbon Canyon Regional Park** on the right. Drive in, pay the small day-use fee, and park in the large lot to the left of the entrance. This is the assumed starting point, though there is limited free parking on the shoulder of Carbon Canyon Road, just east of the regional park.

TRAIL USE
HIke, Run, Bike
LENGTH
12.0 miles, 5 hours
ELEVATION GAIN/LOSS
900'/900'
DIFFICULTY
– 1 2 **3** 4 5 +
TRAIL TYPE
Out & Back
SURFACE TYPE
Dirt

FEATURES
Canyon
Autumn Color
Wildflowers
Birds
Wildlife

Telegraph Canyon

Trail Description

For two centuries, up
until the 1970s, the
Chino Hills were used
for raising cattle and
sheep.

 Canyon

On foot or bike, go back out to the park entrance ▶1 and take the dirt path running east along the shoulder of Carbon Canyon Road. You'll soon see an old ranch road slanting to the right. ▶2 Follow it. This is a back entrance to Chino Hills State Park—the main entrance being several miles east of here off the 71 Freeway in San Bernardino County.

The old ranch road dips in and out of the streambed of **Carbon Canyon**, skirts a citrus grove, and then comes to the base of a hillside. There you pick up the **Telegraph Canyon Trail**, ▶3 an old service road leading east and gradually uphill along the bottom of Telegraph Canyon. Within a few minutes, the sights and sounds of civilization fade, and you'll be pleasantly soothed by the rustle of

More Trails in Chino Hills State Park

OPTIONS

More than 50 miles of dirt roads and old cow paths lace the open ridgelines and thread through the shady canyons of 13,000-acre Chino Hills State Park. Most of these routes are open to mountain bikers, and you will see a fair number of equestrians on them as well. The 1318-foot saddle at the head of Telegraph Canyon is a de facto hub for trails that radiate in every direction. Many possibilities exist for either shortening or lengthening the out-and-back Telegraph Canyon route described in Trail 37.

sycamore leaves, the flutter of birds' wings, and vistas of unspoiled hillsides stretching for miles ahead.

At 5 miles from the start, well up toward the head of the canyon, you'll pass under a cool canopy of huge, gnarled live oaks. Ahead lies an old windmill,▶4 creaking and groaning in the breeze, and a stock pond filled with cattails. Continue climbing to reach a 1318-foot saddle at the very top of Telegraph Canyon.▶5 Here you can stop and enjoy a view stretching many miles to both the east and west.

To complete this outing the simple way, just return the way you came—cruising easily on foot or coasting much of the distance back to Carbon Canyon Regional Park.

The small orange and lemon groves on both sides of Carbon Canyon Road are among the last citrus groves existing in Orange County.

🚶 MILESTONES

▶1   0.0 From Carbon Canyon Regional Park entrance, go east along Carbon Canyon Road

▶2   0.3 Take dirt road slanting to the right

▶3   0.5 Reach mouth of Telegraph Canyon; continue up-canyon on Telegraph Canyon Trail

▶4   5.8 Pass old windmill on the right

▶5   6.0 Arrive at saddle at head of Telegraph Canyon, the turnaround point

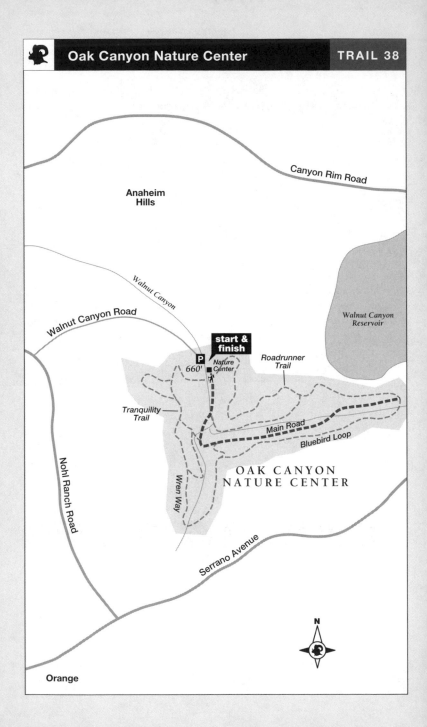

Canyon Rim Road

Anaheim
Hills

Walnut Canyon

Walnut Canyon Road

Walnut Canyon
Reservoir

start &
finish

P 660'

Nature
Center

Roadrunner
Trail

Tranquility
Trail

Main Road

Bluebird Loop

Nohl Ranch Road

Wren Way

OAK CANYON
NATURE CENTER

Serrano Avenue

N

Orange

Oak Canyon Nature Center

Vest-pocket-sized (58-acre) Oak Canyon Nature Center squeezes between a golf course and a reservoir on one side and a suburban housing tract on the other. Small children have plenty of room to roam on the tightly nested, 4 miles' worth of hiking trails here. It's pretty hard for the little ones to get seriously lost, and the price is right—free. For adults, this is a park to savor slowly. Habitats include a trickling stream shaded by coast live oaks, and hillsides coated with chaparral and sage-scrub vegetation.

TRAIL USE
Hike, Run
LENGTH
1 to 2 miles, 1 hour
ELEVATION GAIN/LOSS
200'/200'
DIFFICULTY
– **1** 2 3 4 5 +
TRAIL TYPE
Out & Back
SURFACE TYPE
Dirt

FEATURES
Child Friendly
Handicap Access
Canyon
Wildflowers
Birds
Cool & Shady
Photo Opportunity
Moonlight Hiking

Best Time

The nature center grounds are pleasant all year; in summer you might want to avoid the sunnier trails.

Finding the Trail

To reach Oak Canyon Nature Center from the Riverside Freeway (Highway 91), exit at Imperial Highway and drive 1 mile south to Nohl Ranch Road. Turn left there and go east 2 miles to **Walnut Canyon Road**. Turn left and continue to the end of the road, where you'll find free parking. The center is open 9 A.M. to 5 P.M. No bikes, picnicking, or pets are allowed on the trails.

Trail Description

A few steps from the parking lot will take you to a beautifully rustic interpretive center,▶1 nestled under spreading oaks. There you can view some

Oak Canyon Nature Center serves up a slew of workshops and hikes for families and individuals year round. On certain summer evenings (beyond the normal closing time) the center offers a program called "Nature Nights"—a twilight walk followed by a presentation in the outdoor amphitheater. For more information, call (714) 998-8380.

In a wet year, the wildflowers at Oak Canyon—especially sticky monkeyflower —can be spectacular.

 Wildflowers

exhibits and pick up a detailed trail map. On the grounds of the nature center, numerous short trails diverge from the "Main Road," which is a wide path paralleling a small stream in the bottom of Oak Canyon (a tributary of Walnut Canyon).

You can go about 0.5 mile to the end of the Main Road,▶2 then pick another route for the return. The Stream Trail meanders through the thick of the riparian and oak woodland habitats, while the Roadrunner Ridge and Bluebird trails ascend onto the steep slopes overlooking the ravine bottom. The loop around the outermost perimeter of Oak Canyon Nature Center measures about 2 miles in length.

In summer, you'll find little of interest high on the shadeless, scrub-covered slopes but a lot to enjoy down amid the oaks. In spring, you'll want to gravitate toward the slopes on the south side; this is where a variety of blooming native plants stand shoulder to shoulder.

MILESTONES

▶1 0.0 Start at the nature center building; take Main Road into Oak Canyon

▶2 0.5 End of Main Road; return on Stream Trail, or circle back on canyon rim trails to the left or right

A shady trail *at Oak Canyon Nature Center*

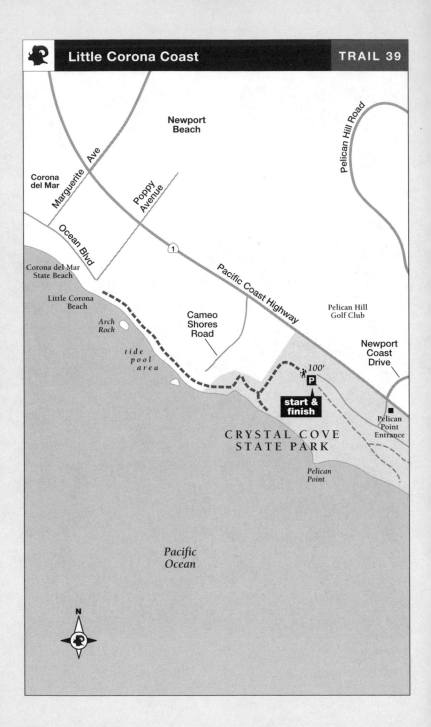

Newport
Beach

Corona
del Mar

Marguerite Ave

Poppy
Avenue

Ocean Blvd

Pelican Hill Road

1

Pacific Coast Highway

Corona del Mar
State Beach

Little Corona
Beach

Arch
Rock

*tide
pool
area*

Cameo
Shores
Road

Pelican Hill
Golf Club

Newport
Coast
Drive

100'

P

start &
finish

CRYSTAL COVE
STATE PARK

Pelican
Point
Entrance

*Pelican
Point*

*Pacific
Ocean*

N

Little Corona Coast

Some of the finest tide pools in Orange County—indeed in all of Southern California—await you on this short, absorbing, and probably time-consuming, rock-hopping trek between the Pelican Point area of Crystal Cove State Park and Little Corona City Beach in Corona del Mar. Wear an old pair of rubber-soled shoes or boots, and expect to get wet below the ankles. Don't turn your back to the incoming waves, otherwise you may get more wet than that.

Best Time

Successful tide pool gazing requires both good light (midafternoon is best) and minus tides. These conditions are satisfied near the time of either new or full moon during the period from October through March. On about 20 afternoons each year, the tide drops to less than 1 foot, which is low enough for you to examine marine life at the lowermost intertidal zone. Plan to start your walk about an hour before predicted low tide.

Finding the Trail

At a point on Pacific Coast Highway 5 miles north of Laguna Beach or 2 miles south of Corona del Mar, turn west into Crystal Cove State Park's **Pelican Point** area. Park hours are variable, depending on the season. After paying the state park day-use fee, stay to the right and drive to the northernmost parking lot on the bluff overlooking the coast.

TRAIL USE
Hike
LENGTH
2.6 miles, 2.5 hours
ELEVATION GAIN/LOSS
100'/100'
DIFFICULTY
- 1 **2** 3 4 5 +
TRAIL TYPE
Out & Back
SURFACE TYPE
Paved trail, rocky shoreline

FEATURES
Child Friendly
Shoreline
Beach
Tide Pools
Photo Opportunity
Geologic Interest

Tide pool at Little Corona Coast

Trail Description

The rock formations in the tide pools and the nearby cliffs are thinly bedded shales, tilted and sometimes fantastically contorted, dating back about 12 million years.

From the parking area, ▶1 a paved bike path—lined with native planted shrubs and spring wildflowers—swings toward the edge of the bluff. The nearly flat bluffs of **Crystal Cove State Park** represent the first (other than the one being cut now at beach level) of several successively higher and older marine terraces extending back into the interior San Joaquin Hills. Over geologic time, there has been both uplift of the land and changes in sea level.

Soon there's a split: left toward the beach, right toward a viewpoint overlooking the ocean. For the rock-hopping trip, descend to the beach ▶2 and turn up-coast over boulders and finlike rock formations into the tide pool area.

On your painstaking way over the rocks toward **Little Corona Beach** you'll pass two picturesque sea stacks just offshore, both pierced by wave action. The northern of the two is named **Arch Rock,** ▶3 but either could just as well have been called "bird rock"

Beach Alternative

OPTIONS

Small kids and folks without a good sense of balance may want to stick to walking on the sandy beach that stretches for several miles (depending on the tide) south of the tide pool area.

for the ever-present pelicans and other avian life.

In the intertidal strip itself, a few dozen steps from high-tide to low-tide level encompass a complete spectrum of marine plants and animals adapted to the various degrees of inundation and exposure. In the high intertidal zone, look for snails, limpets, mussels, crabs, barnacles, and green sea anemones.

✈ **Tidepools**

Closer to the surf, the middle intertidal zone features luxuriant growths of surfgrass and plenty of sea urchins. Mobile creatures here include small fish, shrimp, and the sluglike sea hare.

In the low intertidal zone, many kinds of seaweeds thrive, including the intriguing sea palm. Look for sea urchins, sponges, worms, chitons, snails, sea stars, and hermit crabs. If you're very lucky, an octopus may come your way. Remember that all marine life, shells, and rocks on this coastline are protected.

Go as far as Little Corona Beach ▶4 and then return the same way you came.

🚶 MILESTONES

▶1   0.0 Take paved bike path toward beach
▶2   0.3 Arrive on beach; turn north and follow rocky coastline
▶3   0.9 Pass Arch Rock
▶4   1.3 Reach Little Corona Beach; return by same route

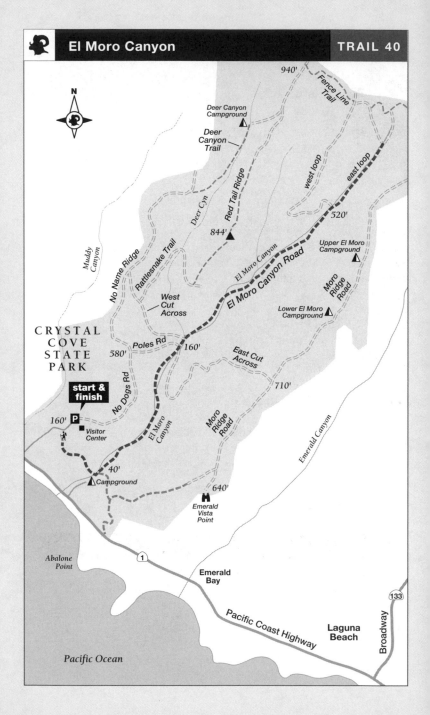

N

940'

Fence Line Trail

Deer Canyon Campground

Deer Canyon Trail

west loop

east loop

Deer Cyn

Red Tail Ridge

520'

844'

Upper El Moro Campground

Muddy Canyon

No Name Ridge

Rattlesnake Trail

El Moro Canyon

El Moro Canyon Road

Moro Ridge Road

West Cut Across

Lower El Moro Campground

CRYSTAL COVE STATE PARK

Poles Rd

580'

160'

East Cut Across

No Dogs Rd

710'

start & finish

160'

P

Visitor Center

El Moro Canyon

Moro Ridge Road

40'

Campground

640'

Emerald Vista Point

Emerald Canyon

Abalone Point

1

Emerald Bay

133

Pacific Coast Highway

Broadway

Laguna Beach

Pacific Ocean

El Moro Canyon

Crystal Cove State Park preserves one of the last large, undisturbed pieces of open space along the Orange County coast. Besides containing a 3-mile stretch of bluffs and ocean front (see Trail 39, p. 209), the park reaches back into the San Joaquin Hills to encompass the entire watershed of El Moro Canyon —over 4 square miles of natural ravines, ridges, and marine terrace formations. The canyon itself is far and away the most beautiful attraction in this backcountry section. Along this out-and-back trek, you'll pass by thickets of willow, toyon, elderberry, and sycamore, all brightly illuminated by the sun; then you'll plunge into cool, dark, cathedral-like recesses overhung by massive limbs of live-oak trees.

TRAIL USE
Hike, Run, Bike
LENGTH
6.8 miles, 3.5 hours
ELEVATION GAIN/LOSS
900'/900'
DIFFICULTY
– 1 **2** 3 4 5 +
TRAIL TYPE
Out & Back
SURFACE TYPE
Dirt

FEATURES
Child Friendly
Canyon
Autumn Colors
Wildflowers
Birds
Cool and Shady
Wildlife

Best Time

Due to its proximity to the coast, El Moro Canyon's temperature is seldom too cool and seldom too hot. Springtime brings eye-popping verdure, and fall furnishes the warm colors of autumn leaves. In the winter, all trails here may temporarily close due to muddy conditions or landslides.

Finding the Trail

From a point on Pacific Coast Highway about 3 miles north of Laguna Beach and 4 miles south of Corona del Mar, turn east onto an access road leading toward **Crystal Cove State Park's** office and **backcountry trailhead**, open 8 a.m. to sunset. Park in the large lot at the end of the access road, and don't forget to pay the day-use parking fee.

Trail Description

Take the trail leading from the parking-lot entrance►1 southwest across a grassy flat and down into shallow **El Moro Canyon**. On the right is a fairly new drive-in campground for the state park. At the bottom you join a wide trail which goes up the canyon.►2 Turn left and walk uphill on the mostly easy gradient.

✔ Canyon

Ascending trails intersect the El Moro Canyon trail on both sides—but you simply stay on the main trail in the canyon bottom. The canyon becomes narrower and more densely wooded in its upper reaches. In one shady recess in the canyon's upper end, several shallow caves, adorned with ferns at their entrances, pock a sandstone outcrop next to the road.

After traveling up the canyon itself for about 3 miles, the trail leaves the lushness of the canyon floor►3 and starts climbing very sharply to a ridge above. This is a good spot to turn around and head back the way you came.

Before the establishment of the California missions, coast-dwelling Indians ate a balanced diet of acorns, seeds, and wild berries from El Moro Canyon and the other coastal canyons, plus abundant marine life.

🚶	MILESTONES
►1	0.0 Follow trail to El Moro Canyon
►2	0.5 Reach bottom of El Moro Canyon, turn left (up-canyon)
►3	3.4 Trail nears head of canyon and begins sharp ascent; good place to turn around and return by same route

El Moro Canyon *in Crystal Cove State Park*

Mountain Biking

NOTICE

The backcountry of Crystal Cove State Park is Orange County's favorite mountain-bike destination. Many loops are possible. Trails range in difficulty: El Moro Canyon is among the easiest.

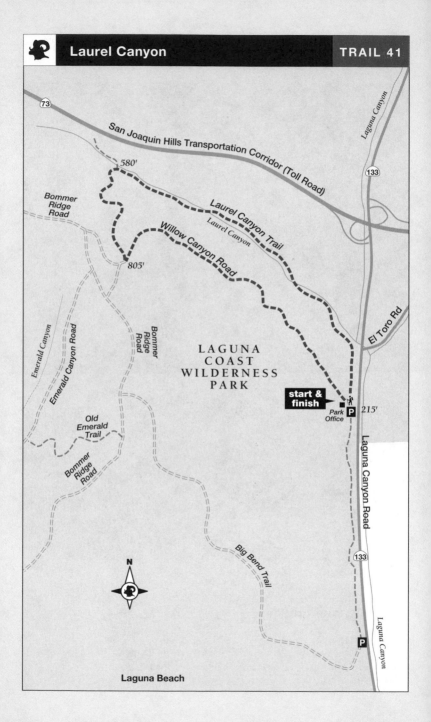

73

San Joaquin Hills Transportation Corridor (Toll Road)

Laguna Canyon

133

580'

Bommer
Ridge
Road

Laurel Canyon Trail

Laurel Canyon

Willow Canyon Road

805'

El Toro Rd

Emerald Canyon

Emerald Canyon Road

Bommer
Ridge
Road

LAGUNA
COAST
WILDERNESS
PARK

Old
Emerald
Trail

Bommer
Ridge
Road

start &
finish

Park
Office

P

215'

Laguna Canyon Road

Big Bend Trail

133

N

P

Laguna Canyon

Laguna Beach

Laurel Canyon

The Laguna Coast Wilderness Park is part of a 19,000-acre patch of protected open space informally known as Orange County's "South Coast Wilderness." Like many scenic and tremendously valuable parcels of property in the pricey county of Orange, this piece was transferred into the public domain in exchange for the former owner's right to develop property elsewhere in the county. For a superb introduction to this gem of a park, try the following 3.5-mile ramble or run into secluded Laurel Canyon.

Best Time

Although temperatures are seldom extreme during any time of year at this coastal location, two seasonal periods stand out: spring, when the landscape is green and dotted with wildflowers; and late fall, when the leaves on the sycamore trees turn golden brown.

Finding the Trail

The place to start is the main trailhead/park office for the Laguna Wilderness Park, on the west side of **Laguna Canyon Road**, 0.7 mile south of the San Joaquin Hills Toll Road (Highway 73). Currently this lot is open 8 A.M. to 4 P.M. on weekends only. The trails within the park may be used 7 A.M. to sunset, on weekends only. Park hours will likely be extended to include weekdays sometime in the future. A small fee is charged for parking your car at the main trailhead.

TRAIL USE
Hike, Run
LENGTH
3.5 miles, 2 hours
ELEVATION GAIN/LOSS
700'/700'
DIFFICULTY
− 1 **2** 3 4 5 +
TRAIL TYPE
Loop
SURFACE TYPE
Dirt

FEATURES
Child Friendly
Canyon
Streams
Waterfall
Autumn Colors
Wildflowers
Birds
Secluded

Trail Description

Centuries ago, many coastal Southern California landscapes such as this were visited by fire just about every decade.

You begin by signing in at a registration table near the office.▶1 You then follow the fire road beyond—the **Willow Canyon Road**, which gains nearly 600 feet of elevation in the next 1.5 miles. Springtime wildflowers bloom in profusion along this stretch, which travels along east and north-facing slopes smothered in thick chaparral vegetation.

At 1.5 miles, turn right on the first intersecting pathway.▶2 Traverse a grassy meadow, and then follow the trail as it plunges down through more dense growths of chaparral toward the narrow bottom of **Laurel Canyon**. As you lose elevation, you also lose sight and sound of the nearby Highway 73 toll road. Once you arrive in the canyon bottom ▶3 (2.0 miles), don't miss the turn onto the narrow trail that branches right and goes down (not up) the canyon. Enjoy the solitude!

OPTIONS

Mountain Biking

Although the narrow, or "single-track" trails in the Laguna Coast Wilderness Park are closed to mountain biking, all fire roads—including the Willow Canyon Road—are open. Detailed trail maps are available at the park office or the registration table.

Graced with gorgeous oaks and sycamores (and copious growths of poison oak), Laurel Canyon is still recovering from the extremely hot and fast-moving Laguna Beach fire of October 1993. At 2.4 miles, you pass near the lip of a dramatic dropoff—a seasonal waterfall,►4 silent except after heavy rains—and swing to the left side of the canyon bottom. You descend along a dry, south-facing slope, and by 3.0 miles emerge in a grassy meadow,►5 which is either green, golden, or transitional in color, depending on the season. Cavernous sandstone outcrops dot the meadow on the left and the slope on the right. The shapes of some suggest grotesque skulls and other figures. The path through the meadow soon flanks busy Laguna Canyon Road, and you arrive back at your parked car.►6

 Canyon

𝕀	MILESTONES
►1	0.0 From trailhead follow Willow Canyon fire road uphill
►2	1.5 Turn right on first intersecting trail; descend into canyon
►3	2.0 Reach canyon floor; go downhill through canyon
►4	2.4 Pass top of seasonal waterfall
►5	3.0 Emerge from canyon and enter meadow
►6	3.5 Return to trailhead

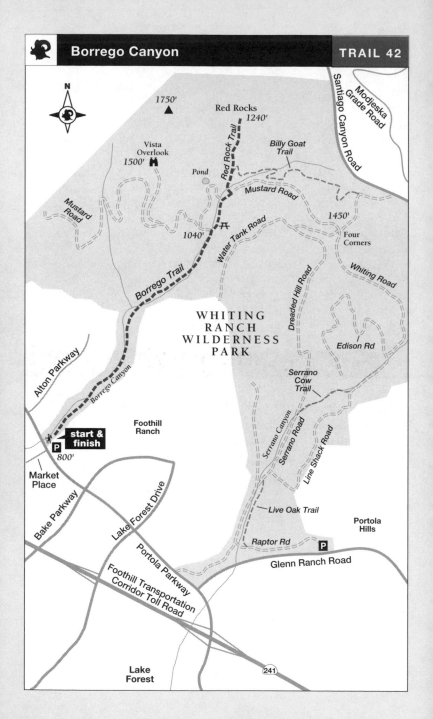

1750'

Red Rocks
1240'

Modjeska Grade Road

Santiago Canyon Road

Vista Overlook
1500'

Billy Goat Trail

Pond

Red Rock Trail

Mustard Road

Mustard Road

1040'

Water Tank Road

1450'

Four Corners

Whiting Road

Borrego Trail

Dreaded Hill Road

WHITING RANCH WILDERNESS PARK

Edison Rd

Serrano Cow Trail

Alton Parkway

Borrego Canyon

Foothill Ranch

Serrano Canyon

Serrano Road

Line Shack Road

start & finish
800'

Market Place

Bake Parkway

Lake Forest Drive

Live Oak Trail

Portola Hills

Raptor Rd

Portola Parkway

Glenn Ranch Road

Foothill Transportation Corridor Toll Road

Lake Forest

241

Borrego Canyon

Whiting Ranch Wilderness Park, a county-run facility on the rim of the suburbs of Lake Forest and El Toro, offers an instant escape from urban world. On your way through Borrego Canyon, you follow an oak-shaded recess into the higher and drier hills, and finally come upon the Red Rocks—a natural amphitheater with eroded sandstone cliffs optimistically referred to as Orange County's "Little Grand Canyon."

TRAIL USE
Hike, Run
LENGTH
4.0 miles, 2 hours
ELEVATION GAIN/LOSS
500'/500'
DIFFICULTY
- 1 **2** 3 4 5 +
TRAIL TYPE
Out & Back
SURFACE TYPE
Dirt

FEATURES
Dogs Allowed
Child Friendly
Canyon
Stream
Waterfall
Cool & Shady
Photo Opportunity
Geologic Interest

Best Time

Any time of year is fine, though the stream in Borrego Canyon runs best in the late winter and early spring.

Finding the Trail

To reach the park's main entrance from Interstate 5 in southern Orange County, take Lake Forest Drive east and north for 5 miles to Portola Parkway, turn left, and follow Portola northwest for another ¹/₂ mile. Look for a trailhead parking area on the right, just beyond a shopping center. The lot is open from 7 A.M. to sunset. If you are using the Foothill Transportation Corridor (Highway 241) toll road, exit at either Lake Forest Drive or Portola Parkway.

Trail Description

Using the Borrego Trail▶1 you immediately plunge into densely shaded **Borrego Canyon**, alongside a stream that happily trickles through during winter and spring. For a while, suburbia rims the canyon

221

Oaks *in Borrego Canyon*

Canyon

on both sides, but soon enough it disappears without a trace. The trek up the canyon feels Tolkienesque as you pass under a crooked-limb canopy of live oaks and sycamores, and sniff the damp odor of the streamside willows. After no more than about 40 minutes of walking and 1.3 miles, you come to **Mustard Road,**▶2 a fire road that ascends both east and west to ridgetops offering long views of the ocean on clear days. Turn right on Mustard Road, pass a picnic site, and take the second trail to the left▶3 (the **Red Rock Trail**—for hikers only), into an upper tributary of Borrego Canyon.

Out in the sunshine now, you meander up the bottom of a sunny ravine that becomes increasingly narrow and steep. Presently, you reach the base of the eroded sandstone cliffs,▶4 formed of sediment deposited on a shallow sea bottom about 20 million years ago. This type of rock, which contains the fossilized remains of shellfish and marine mammals, underlies much of Orange County. Rarely is it as well exposed as here.

Photographers come to **Red Rocks** late in the day, when the setting sun's warm glow brings out the ruddy tint of oxidized iron in the sandstone.

Often in the late fall and winter, frigid air sinks into Borrego Canyon overnight, and by early morning frost mantles everything below eye-level.

🚶	**MILESTONES**	
▶1	0.0	Take the Borrego Trail up Borrego Canyon
▶2	1.3	Intersection of Mustard fire road; turn right
▶3	1.6	Turn left on narrow Red Rock Trail
▶4	2.0	Arrive at Red Rocks; return by the same route

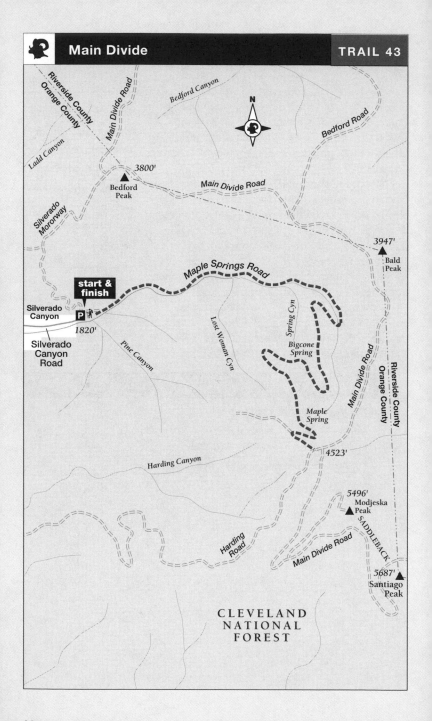

Bedford Canyon

Riverside County
Orange County

Main Divide Road

Bedford Road

N

Ladd Canyon

Silverado Mororway

3800'
▲
Bedford Peak

Main Divide Road

3947'
▲
Bald Peak

Maple Springs Road

start & finish

Silverado Canyon

P

1820'

Silverado Canyon Road

Pine Canyon

Lost Woman Cyn

Spring Cyn

Bigcone Spring

Maple Spring

Main Divide Road

Riverside County
Orange County

4523'

Harding Canyon

5496'
▲
Modjeska Peak

SADDLEBACK

Harding Road

Main Divide Road

5687'
▲
Santiago Peak

CLEVELAND
NATIONAL
FOREST

Main Divide

The Main Divide (summit ridge) of the Santa Ana Mountains is the goal of this twisty, gradually ascending route through chaparral and pines. It's a lengthy and possibly tedious trek for hikers, a heart-pumping cruise for mountain bikers, and a significant challenge for long-distance runners. Do it on a clear, crisp winter day to take advantage of a sweeping view that includes much of coastal Southern California.

TRAIL USE
Hike, Run, Bike
LENGTH
14.0 miles, 7 hours
ELEVATION GAIN/LOSS
2700'/2700'
DIFFICULTY
− 1 2 3 **4** 5 +
TRAIL TYPE
Out and Back
SURFACE TYPE
Paved, Dirt

Best Time

Cool weather is by far the best, as much of the route is open to full sunlight. In recent years the route has been closed to all recreational use between April and September to protect the habitat of the endangered arroyo toad. Call Cleveland National Forest's Trabuco District office at (909) 736-1811 for information about possible closures.

FEATURES
Handicap Access
Dogs Allowed
Canyon
Mountain
Autumn Colors
Wildflowers
Birds
Wildlife
Great Views

Finding the Trail

From the Eastern Transportation Corridor Toll Roads (either Highway 241 or 261) in eastern Orange County, exit at Santiago Canyon Road and drive east 6 miles to Silverado Canyon Road, on the left.

Turn there and continue driving east into Silverado Canyon, straight though the rustic canyon community of Silverado. At 5.4 miles from Santiago Canyon Road you arrive at a vehicle turnaround and parking area, right at the edge of Cleveland National Forest.

Maple Springs Road

Trail Description

Autumn Colors

Proceed past the vehicle gate ▶1 (usually closed and locked so as to block motorized vehicles), and into the higher reaches of Silverado Canyon, which is graced with a small stream. The road you are on, now called **Maple Springs Road**, is thinly paved for the first three miles, ▶2 then dirt for the next four miles.

The 7-mile ascent is a botanist's dream, starting with riparian vegetation: sycamore, alders, and bigleaf maples. Next, in the somewhat higher and drier ravines, comes oak woodland: live oaks, bigcone Douglas-fir, bay laurels, and more maples. Finally, past the end of the pavement, the dirt road ascends dry slopes smothered in thick carpets of manzanita shrubs dotted with sturdy Coulter pines.

After climbing for 7 miles, you come to a complex intersection of dirt roads ▶3 north of, and about 1000 vertical feet below, imposing **Modjeska Peak**. This is where several popular hiking/mountain biking routes come together in a 100-yard space: **Harding Road**, two branches of **Main Divide Road**, and of course Maple Springs Road.

Modjeska Peak and **Santiago Peak** to the south of the intersection together make up what is known as Saddleback, Orange County's highest mountain and a familiar feature on the county's eastern horizon. It is not necessary to climb either of the two antenna-dotted peaks. Views in all directions except south are almost as good from high ground near the intersection of roads. At best, the view—from the Pacific coast to the San Jacinto Mountains—is stupendous.

Your return to the starting point is back by way of Maple Springs Road—entirely downhill, but never too steeply.

A plaque at the Silverado parking area tells of Cañada de la Madera (Timber Canyon), the original name for Silverado Canyon.

 Great Views

🚶	**MILESTONES**
▶1	0.0 From east end of Silverado community, take Maple Springs Road
▶2	3.0 Oiled road ends; dirt road continues
▶3	7.0 Intersection of several dirt roads atop Main Divide; a good place to enjoy the view before heading back

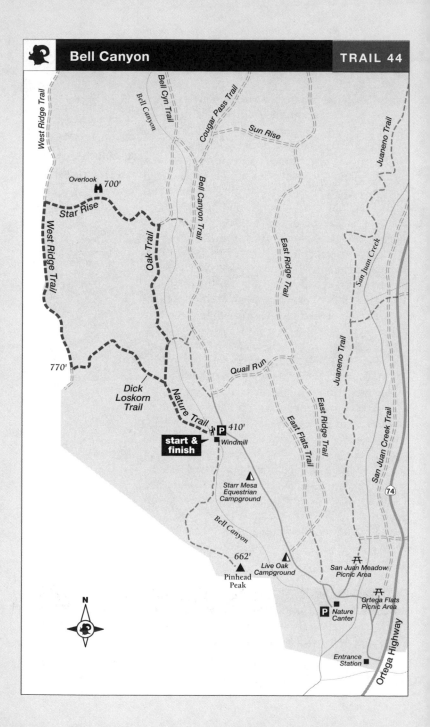

West Ridge Trail

Bell Canyon

Bell Cyn Trail

Cougar Pass Trail

Sun Rise

Juaneno Trail

Overlook 700'

Star Rise

Oak Trail

West Ridge Trail

Bell Canyon Trail

East Ridge Trail

San Juan Creek

770'

Quail Run

Juaneno Trail

Dick Loskorn Trail

Nature Trail

San Juan Creek Trail

start & finish

P 410'

Windmill

East Flats Trail

East Ridge Trail

74

Starr Mesa Equestrian Campground

Bell Canyon

662'

Live Oak Campground

San Juan Meadow Picnic Area

Pinhead Peak

Ortega Flats Picnic Area

N

P Nature Center

Entrance Station

Ortega Highway

Bell Canyon

Caspers Wilderness Park is Orange County's largest county park (8000 acres), the least altered by humans, and the most remote from population centers. This hike showcases the finest features of the Santa Ana Mountain foothills. You'll climb the sandstone-ribbed wall of Bell Canyon, enjoy some views of Orange County's remaining rural and wild areas, and finally descend to Bell Canyon's floor for a good look at fine specimens of live oak and sycamores.

Best Time

Caspers is primarily a three-season park, generally too warm and dry between July and September, and far more beautiful and comfortable during November through April. Muddy conditions after a winter storm may close the trails for a period of up to several days.

Finding the Trail

From Interstate 5 at San Juan Capistrano, drive east on Ortega Highway (Highway 74) 7.6 miles to the park entrance on the left, where you pay a fee to enter. Day-use hours are 7 A.M. to sunset daily. Drive in past the nature center and continue 1 mile up Bell Canyon on a paved road to a parking lot at the old windmill—a local point of interest and reference point for the trail system.

Trail Description

Begin hiking at the old windmill▶1 on a path designated "Nature Trail." Follow it across the wide bed

TRAIL USE
Hike, Run
LENGTH
3.5 miles, 2 hours
ELEVATION GAIN/LOSS
400'/400'
DIFFICULTY
– 1 **2** 3 4 5 +
TRAIL TYPE
Loop
SURFACE TYPE
Dirt

FEATURES
Child Friendly
Canyon
Autumn Colors
Wildflowers
Birds
Wildlife
Great Views

of Bell Canyon and into the dense oak woodland on the far side. After 0.3 mile, you'll spot a park bench beneath a gorgeous, spreading oak tree. A little farther on, veer left on the **Dick Loskorn Trail**.►2 This narrow path meanders up a shallow draw and soon climbs to a sandstone ridgeline that at one point narrows to near-knife-edge width. At one point you'll find yourself stepping within a foot of a modest but unnerving abyss.

The sandstone outcrops along the Dick Loskorn Trail belong to the Santiago Formation, which can be seen in many places throughout the coastal hills of Orange County. The sandstone originates from sediments laid down about 45 million years ago.

After climbing about 350 feet, you reach a dirt

🐦 **Birds**

Windmill in Caspers Wilderness Park

OPTIONS

Further Exploring

Don't miss a stop at the visitor center, which contains a small museum and an open-air loft offering an expansive view of the Santa Ana Mountains.

Caspers Wilderness Park offers a good selection of old ranch roads suitable (and legal) for mountain bike riding. Most of these bike-suitable trails go up the ridges to the east of Bell Canyon.

road—the **West Ridge Trail**. Turn right (north),►3 skirting the fence line of Rancho Mission Viejo, a vast landholding that encompasses much of southern Orange County. Before World War II, it included all of Camp Pendleton as well. To the left you look down on a broad, shallow canyon known as Cañada Gobernadora, which is gradually being overtaken by luxury housing.

After 0.7 mile on the West Ridge Trail, turn right on the trail named **Star Rise**.►4 You descend back into Bell Canyon, this time on a wider path. Nearing the bottom, veer right on the Oak Trail.►5 On this delightful trace of the trail, you'll meander past California sycamores as well as ancient coast live oaks. Sunlight filtering through the sycamore leaves bathes the ground shadows in a jungle-green luminance. The **Oak Trail**►6 will return you to the Nature Trail, and then your starting point.►7

Autumn Colors

🚶 MILESTONES

►1	0.0	From windmill follow Nature Trail
►2	0.4	Turn left on Dick Loskorn Trail; ascend sharply
►3	1.0	Reach top of ridge; turn right on West Ridge Trail
►4	1.7	Turn right on Star Rise and descend
►5	2.4	Turn right on Oak Trail
►6	3.0	Join Nature Trail; keep straight
►7	3.5	Return to windmill

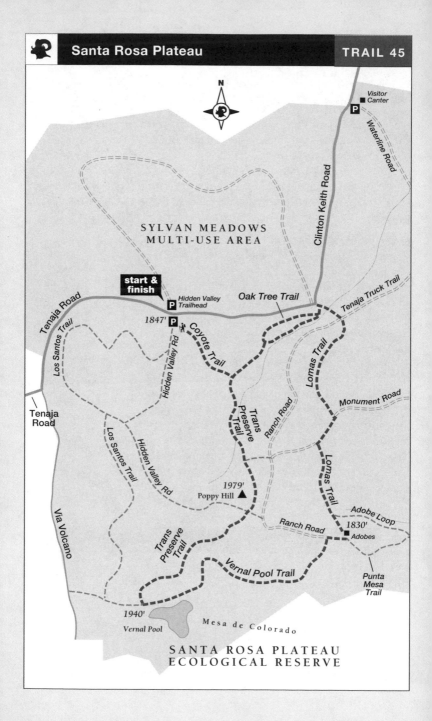

N

SYLVAN MEADOWS
MULTI-USE AREA

Visitor
Canter

Clinton Keith Road

Waterline Road

start &
finish

Hidden Valley
Trailhead

Oak Tree Trail

Tenaja Truck Trail

Tenaja Road

Los Santos Trail

1847'

Hidden Valley Rd

Coyote Trail

Lomas Trail

Tenaja
Road

Los Santos Trail

Hidden Valley Rd

Trans
Preserve
Trail

Ranch Road

Monument Road

Lomas Trail

1979'
Poppy Hill

Via Volcano

Trans
Preserve
Trail

Ranch Road

Adobe Loop

1830'

Adobes

Punta
Mesa
Trail

Vernal Pool Trail

1940'

Vernal Pool

Mesa de Colorado

SANTA ROSA PLATEAU
ECOLOGICAL RESERVE

Santa Rosa Plateau

The Santa Rosa Plateau Ecological Reserve serves up a classic California landscape of wind-rippled grasses, swaying poppies, statuesque oak trees, trickling streams, vernal pools, and a dazzling assortment of native plants (nearly 500 at last count) and animals. Your visit to the 8300-acre reserve takes you outside the boundary of Orange County and into the fast-growing southeastern corner of Riverside County, but you'll feel like you're far away from the people-packed suburbs.

Best Time

Every Southern Californian should have at least one chance to see the Santa Rosa Plateau Reserve at its stunning best—during March and April, following a wet winter. The wildflowers are eye-popping, the large vernal pool is filled to the brim, and the rolling, emerald-green hills will make you think you've found paradise. Due to the reserve's often-hot, inland locale, summer visits are worthwhile only during early morning or early evening hours.

Finding the Trail

Follow Interstate 15 south of Corona to the Clinton Keith Road exit in Murrieta. Drive south on Clinton Keith Road, passing the reserve's visitor center (open weekends) at 5 miles. Keep going, and note the sharp rightward bend at 6 miles where the road's name changes to Tenaja Road. At 0.7 mile past this sharp bend, park at the Hidden Valley Trailhead parking area (on either side of the road). There's a

TRAIL USE
Hike, Run, Bike
LENGTH
6.0 miles, 2.5 hours
ELEVATION GAIN/LOSS
400'/400'
DIFFICULTY
– 1 **2** 3 4 5 +
TRAIL TYPE
Loop
SURFACE TYPE
Dirt

FEATURES
Dogs Allowed
Child Friendly
Canyon
Autumn Colors
Wildflowers
Birds
Wildlife
Cool & Shady
Great Views
Photo Opportunity
Historic
Geologic Interest

Wildflowers

small day-use fee, payable here. Trails in the reserve are open from sunrise to sunset.

Trail Description

The 6-mile loop hike outlined here will give you a comprehensive look at the reserve's best features. From the **Hidden Valley Trailhead,**▶1 head south-east on the **Coyote Trail**. After 0.5 mile, turn right on the **Trans Preserve Trail.**▶2 Follow it for 1.5 miles over rolling and sometimes wooded terrain, passing through part of the reserve's 3000 acres of remnant native "bunchgrass prairie." Reserve managers have been implementing controlled burns here to discourage the growth of nonnative grasses and encourage the recovery of native plants.

The last half mile of the Trans Preserve Trail rises to a plateau called **Mesa de Colorado**. At the top of the mesa, you turn left on the **Vernal Pool Trail**▶3 and soon visit one of the largest vernal pools in California ▶4 (39 acres at maximum capacity). The hard-pan surface underneath vernal pools is quite impervious to water, so once filled during winter storms, the pools can dry out only by evaporation. Unusual and sometimes unique species of flowering plants have evolved around the perimeter of this and other vernal pools throughout the state.

Continue east on the Vernal Pool Trail, and descend from Mesa de Colorado to the two adobe buildings of the former Santa Rosa Ranch,▶5 3.3

Visitor Center

OPTIONS

Visit the Santa Rosa Plateau Ecological Reserve visitor center, open Saturday and Sunday, 9 A.M. to 5 P.M., for more information on the reserve's natural history and trails. A fraction of the reserve's trails, especially north of the visitor center and in the recently acquired Sylvan Meadows area, are open to mountain biking.

miles from the start. Constructed around 1845, these are Riverside County's oldest standing structures.

After a look at the adobes and a refreshing pause in the shade, make a beeline north on the Lomas Trail. You'll jog briefly right on Monument Road, ▶6 then go left to stay on the Lomas Trail. At the junction with Tenaja Truck Trail ahead, ▶7 go straight across toward the looping **Oak Tree Trail**. The left (streamside) branch is better—assuming the creek is flowing.

Autumn Colors

Both alternatives give you a close-up look at some of the finest Engelmann-oak woodland anywhere. The Engelmann oak tree, with its distinctive gray-green leaves, is endemic to a narrow strip of coastal foothills stretching from Southern California into northern Baja California. It is becoming one of the rarer of the state's oak species, primarily because its native range is squarely in the path of current and future suburban and rural development.

At the far end of the Oak Tree Trail loop, you come to the Trans Preserve Trail. ▶8 Use it to reach the Coyote Trail, ▶9 where a right turn and a retracing of earlier steps takes you a final half mile to your starting point. ▶10

🚶 MILESTONES

▶1	0.0	From Hidden Valley Trailhead, follow Coyote Trail
▶2	0.5	Turn right on Trans Preserve Trail
▶3	2.0	Turn left on Vernal Pool Trail
▶4	2.2	Pass Vernal Pool
▶5	3.3	Visit historic Santa Rosa Ranch adobes; take Lomas Trail north
▶6	3.9	Jog briefly right on Monument Road, then go left on Lomas Trail
▶7	4.7	Cross Tenaja Truck Trail; follow Oak Tree Trail
▶8	5.2	Meet Trans-Preserve Trail; continue southwest
▶9	5.5	Reach Coyote Trail, turn right
▶10	6.0	Arrive at Hidden Valley Trailhead

San Bernardino/ San Jacinto Mountains

San Bernardino/
San Jacinto Mountains

By any standard, the San Bernardino and San Jacinto mountain ranges are giants. Both rise from the lowland valleys of 2000 feet elevation or less, to cloud-scraping heights of more than 10,000 feet. From the base of San Jacinto Mountains at Palm Springs to the San Jacinto Peak summit, there is an amazing 2 miles of vertical relief!

These two mountain ranges are somewhat remote from all but the easternmost fringe of the L.A. metropolitan area, but they attract like magnets anyone interested in the challenges of high-altitude hiking. Only three trails comprise this chapter; one each will get you to the highest peaks in Southern California, while the third starts near the shore of the perennially favorite Big Bear Lake.

Permits and Maps

All three trails in this chapter lie within the San Bernardino National Forest. For parking purposes, a National Forest Adventure Pass (see the introduction to the San Gabriel Mountains chapter, p. 111 for complete information) is required for the first two trails.

Both San Gorgonio Mountain and San Jacinto Peak lie within designated wilderness areas, and both require wilderness permits for all entry, both day and overnight. Each trail writeup gives full details.

The San Bernardino National Forest recreation map, available from the forest service and certain outdoor retailers, shows roads, trails, and public-private property boundaries in the region that includes the two mountain ranges. Detailed trail maps for both San Gorgonio Mountain and San Jacinto Peak are available for purchase at the ranger stations where you will likely pick up your wilderness permit for these areas.

For driving purposes, the Automobile Club of Southern California's *Los Angeles and Orange Counties and Vicinity* map is highly recommended—as it is for the entire region covered by this book.

San Bernardino/ San Jacinto Mountains

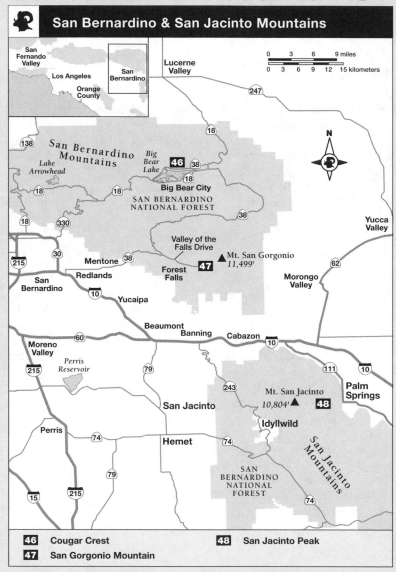

San Bernardino & San Jacinto Mountains

San Fernando Valley

Los Angeles

San Bernardino

Orange County

Lucerne Valley

0   3   6   9 miles
0   3   6   9   12   15 kilometers

247

138

18

San Bernardino Mountains

Lake Arrowhead

Big Bear Lake

46   38

18

Big Bear City

SAN BERNARDINO NATIONAL FOREST

18

18

38

N

Yucca Valley

18

330

Valley of the Falls Drive

38

47   ▲ Mt. San Gorgonio 11,499'

62

Mentone

Redlands

Forest Falls

Morongo Valley

215

30

San Bernardino

10

Yucaipa

Beaumont   Banning   Cabazon

10

Moreno Valley

60

215

Perris Reservoir

79

243

111

10

Mt. San Jacinto 10,804' ▲   **48**

Palm Springs

San Jacinto

Idyllwild

Perris

74

Hemet

74

San Jacinto Mountains

79

SAN BERNARDINO NATIONAL FOREST

15

215

74

46   Cougar Crest   **48**   San Jacinto Peak
47   San Gorgonio Mountain

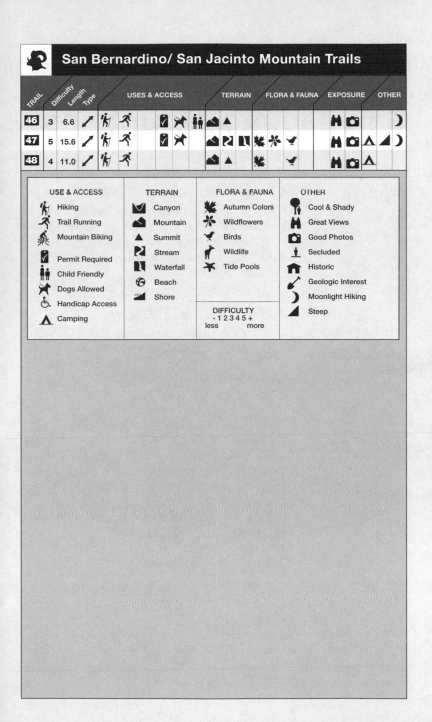

TRAIL	Difficulty	Length	Type	USES & ACCESS	TERRAIN	FLORA & FAUNA	EXPOSURE	OTHER
46	3	6.6						
47	5	15.6						
48	4	11.0						

USE & ACCESS
- Hiking
- Trail Running
- Mountain Biking
- Permit Required
- Child Friendly
- Dogs Allowed
- Handicap Access
- Camping

TERRAIN
- Canyon
- Mountain
- Summit
- Stream
- Waterfall
- Beach
- Shore

FLORA & FAUNA
- Autumn Colors
- Wildflowers
- Birds
- Wildlife
- Tide Pools

DIFFICULTY
- 1 2 3 4 5 +
less   more

OTHER
- Cool & Shady
- Great Views
- Good Photos
- Secluded
- Historic
- Geologic Interest
- Moonlight Hiking
- Steep

San Bernardino/
San Jacinto Mountains

Stone hut *atop San Jacinto Peak (Trail 48)*

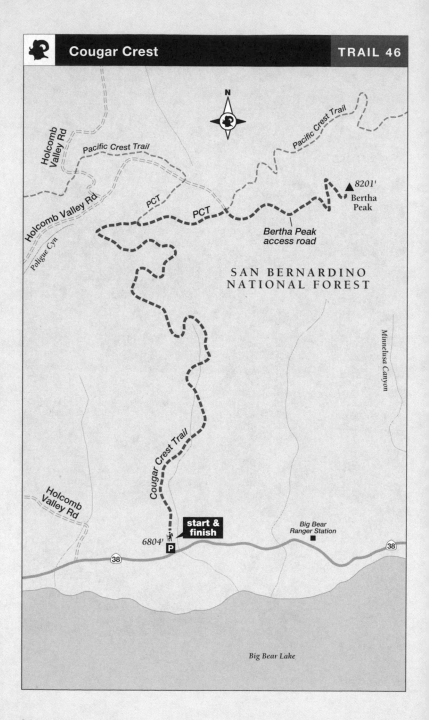

N

Holcomb Valley Rd

Pacific Crest Trail

Holcomb Valley Rd

Poligue Cyn

PCT

PCT

Pacific Crest Trail

8201'
Bertha
Peak

*Bertha Peak
access road*

SAN BERNARDINO
NATIONAL FOREST

Minnelusa Canyon

Cougar Crest Trail

Holcomb
Valley Rd

**start &
finish**

6804'

P

38

Big Bear
Ranger Station

38

Big Bear Lake

Cougar Crest

Big Bear Lake, popular with Southlanders, offers snow sports in the winter, boating and fishing in the summer, and hiking, mountain biking, and trail running during the warmer half of the year. The Cougar Crest route, which rises above the lake's serene north shore, takes you to a high point where your gaze encompasses the rounded peaks of the San Bernardino Mountains, and the vast Mojave Desert.

Best Time

The first 2 miles (Cougar Crest Trail portion) of the route lies on a south-facing slope that often becomes snow-free in March or April. Beyond this point, on north-facing slopes, hard-packed, slippery snowbanks may cover the trail until sometime in May. Late spring through late fall is usually the best time.

Finding the Trail

If you are arriving at Big Bear by way of Highways 330 and 18 from San Bernardino (the most common approach), turn left on Highway 38 as soon as you reach Big Bear Lake, and drive along the north shore for 5 miles to the large **Cougar Crest trailhead** on the left. This same trailhead is located 4 miles west of Big Bear City via Highway 38. Be sure to display your National Forest Adventure Pass.

Trail Description

Start by heading up the **Cougar Crest Trail,**▶1 formerly an obscure dirt road. Traces of mining activity

TRAIL USE
Hike, Run
LENGTH
6.6 miles, 3.5 hours
ELEVATION GAIN/LOSS
1450'/1450'
DIFFICULTY
– 1 2 **3** 4 5 +
TRAIL TYPE
Out & Back
SURFACE TYPE
Dirt

FEATURES
Permit Required
Dogs Allowed
Child Friendly
Mountain
Summit
Great Views
Photo Opportunity
Moonlight Hiking

245

▲ Summit

are evident as you climb upward along a shallow draw filled with a photogenic mix of outsized pinyon pines and junipers, and occasional straight and tall Jeffrey pines.

After a long mile, the old road becomes a narrow trail▶2 and begins to curl and switchback along higher and sunnier slopes. **Big Bear Lake** comes into view occasionally, its surface azure in the slanting illumination of a spring or summer morning, or dotted with silvery pinpoints of light on a late fall day.

After about 2 miles, the trail reaches a divide,▶3 bends right, and for a short distance traverses a cool (or sometimes cold and icy), north-facing slope. At 2.2 miles, the Cougar Crest Trail hooks up with the **Pacific Crest Trail.**▶4 Bear right and start contouring east, high on the sunny, south-facing slope. Spread before you now is the lake—which half-fills a 10-mile-long trough in the mountains—and various resort and residential communities spread along the shore and beyond.

When the PCT crosses a rock-strewn service road▶5 (2.6 miles from the start), leave the nicely graded trail and start climbing east on the road. A steep, 0.7-mile ascent takes you to a small microwave relay station atop **Bertha Peak.**▶6 Here you'll find a peak bagger's register, plus fine views over the treetops and into the Mojave Desert to the north.

🚶	MILESTONES	
▶1	0.0	Follow the Cougar Crest Trail
▶2	1.1	Trail narrows, starts crooked ascent
▶3	2.0	Trail crosses from south side to north side of ridge
▶4	2.2	Junction with Pacific Crest Trail; bear right
▶5	2.6	Trail crosses dirt service road; turn right and climb
▶6	3.3	Arrive at Bertha Peak summit; return by same route

Mountain Biking

OPTIONS

Mountain bikes are allowed on the Cougar Crest Trail, but not permitted on any part of the Pacific Crest Trail. This prohibition is of little consequence to mountain bikers, who are free to enjoy an extensive network of fire roads and smaller trails on the slopes both north and south of Big Bear Lake. More information can be obtained at the San Bernardino National Forest ranger station just east of the Cougar Crest trailhead.

Cougar Crest Trail traverses a botanical melding of high-desert pinyon-juniper woodland and montane Jeffrey-pine forest.

Sugar pine

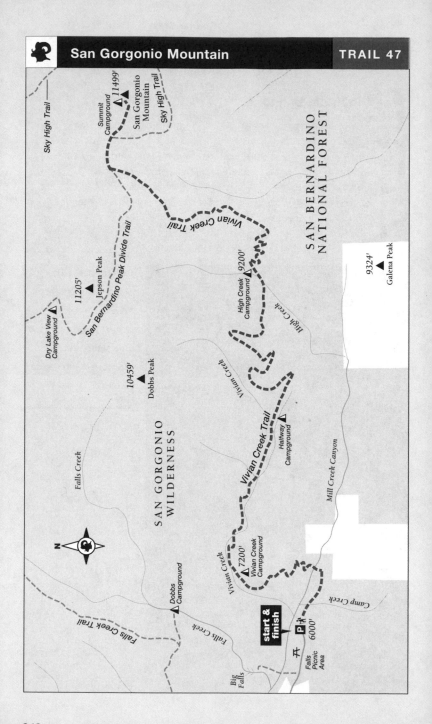

Sky High Trail

Summit Campground

11499'
San Gorgonio Mountain

Sky High Trail

SAN BERNARDINO NATIONAL FOREST

Vivian Creek Trail

11205'
Jepson Peak

San Bernardino Peak Divide Trail

Dry Lake View Campground

High Creek Campground 9200'

9324'
Galena Peak

High Creek

10459'
Dobbs Peak

Vivian Creek

SAN GORGONIO WILDERNESS

Falls Creek

Vivian Creek Trail

Halfway Campground

Mill Creek Canyon

N

Dobbs Campground

7200'
Vivian Creek Campground

Vivian Creek

Camp Creek

Falls Creek Trail

start & finish

P

6000'

Falls Picnic Area

Big Falls

San Gorgonio Mountain

Bagging the barren, 11,499-foot summit of San Gorgonio Mountain, the highest elevation in California south of the Sierra Nevada, is a quintessential accomplishment for L.A.-area hikers. The century-old Vivian Creek Trail route to the top from the south is the shortest of about eight distinct routes or variations; even so, it's never an easy task. Some people backpack the 15.6-mile round-trip distance in two or three days. Fit dayhikers clock in at 10 hours or less, and highly trained mountain runners may cut even that time in half.

Best Time

The hiking season on the Vivian Creek Trail begins in May of June, when the trail becomes snow free. June and early July normally feature clear, though often uncomfortably warm weather. From Mid-July through early September, afternoon thunderstorms visit the higher elevations with some regularity. Calm weather returns, and cool temperatures prevail, from late September through November. Sometime in November or December, the window for easy hiking closes with the first cold storm of the winter season. At a slower hiking pace, you may need 12 to 14 hours in all for a one-day hike—which means (in the fall season at least) you should begin well before sunrise.

Finding the Trail

From Interstate 10 just east of the city of San Bernardino, exit at Highway 38 (Orange Street) in

TRAIL USE
Hike, Run

LENGTH
15.6 miles, 10 hours

ELEVATION GAIN/LOSS
5700'/5700'

DIFFICULTY
– 1 2 3 4 **5** +

TRAIL TYPE
Out & Back

SURFACE TYPE
Dirt

FEATURES
Permit Required
Dogs Allowed
Canyon
Mountain
Summit
Streams
Waterfall
Autumn Colors
Wildflowers
Birds
Great Views
Photo Opportunity
Camping
Moonlight Hiking
Steep

Hikers enjoy the view *atop San Gorgonio Mountain*

Redlands. Turn left (north), proceed 0.5 mile north to Lugonia Avenue, and turn right (east), remaining on Highway 38. Continue 8 miles to an intersection with Bryant Street. The Mill Creek Ranger Station, where you can secure the necessary wilderness permit for hiking the Vivian Creek Trail, is located at this intersection. Opening hours vary according to season, and some permits may be available by self-registration outside the station's door early in the morning. Call (909) 794-1123 for more information. Back on the road again, continue driving east on Highway 38, now signed Mill Creek Road, for 6.2 miles. Turn right at Valley of the Falls Boulevard, and proceed the remaining 4.3 miles to the roadend, where a large paved parking lot, the Vivian Creek Trailhead, accommodates forest visitors (with a National Forest Adventure Pass, of course).

Trail Description

From the **Vivian Creek Trailhead1,▶1** walk east (uphill) past a vehicle gate and follow a dirt road for 0.6 mile to its end▶2. Go left across the wide, boulder wash of Mill Creek and find the **Vivian Creek Trail▶3** going sharply up the oak-clothed canyon wall on the far side. The next half mile is excruciatingly steep (it's worse on the return, when your weary quadriceps muscles must absorb the punishment of each lurching downhill step).

Mercifully, at the top of this steep section, the trail levels momentarily, then assumes a moderate grade up alongside Vivian Creek.▶4 A sylvan Shangri-La unfolds ahead. Pines, firs, and cedars reach for the sky. Bracken fern smothers the banks of the melodious creek, which dances over boulders and fallen trees.

 Stream

Near **Halfway Campground ▶5** (2.5 miles) you begin climbing timber-dotted slopes covered intermittently by thickets of manzanita. After several zigs and zags on shady north-facing slopes, you swing onto a brightly illuminated south-facing slope. Serrated Yucaipa Ridge looms in the south, rising sheer from the depths of Mill Creek Canyon. Soon thereafter, the sound of bubbling water heralds your arrival at **High Creek ▶6** (4.8 miles) and the trail camp of the same name.

 Camping

Past the High Creek camp the trail ascends gently on several long switchback segments through lodgepole pines, and attains a saddle on a rocky ridge. The pines thin out and appear more decrepit

OPTIONS

Nearby Mountain Biking Trails

Due to its status as a federal wilderness area, mountain bike travel is prohibited in the San Gorgonio Mountain area above about 7000 feet elevation. Mountain bicyclists will find plenty of roads and trails in the Big Bear area a few miles north, however.

as you climb crookedly up along this ridge toward timberline. At 7.2 miles, the **San Bernardino Peak Divide Trail** intersects from the left.▶7 Stay right and keep climbing on a moderate grade across stony slopes dotted with cowering, stunted pines shaped by gales, smothering snow, and months-long droughts. Soon, nearly all vegetation disappears.

On the right you pass **Sky High Trail,**▶8 which curls up the mountain slope from the east. Keep straight, and don't give up! A final burst of effort puts you on a boulder pile marking the highest elevation in Southern California ▶9 (7.8 miles from your starting point). From this vantage, even the soaring north face of San Jacinto Peak to the south appears diminished in stature. On the clearest days the Pacific Ocean appears in the southwest, and the northern view may include Telescope Peak, 180 miles away, in Death Valley National Park.

 Great Views

When it's time to leave, do a few leg-stretching exercises first to limber up. The return is relentlessly and at times jarringly downhill.

Other Routes to the Summit

Two other popular routes to Gorgonio's summit come from the north via Dollar Lake and Dry Lake. From the nearest north-side trailhead, each of these (or a loop involving both) involves less elevation gain than the Vivian Creek route, and a round-trip distance of well over 20 miles.

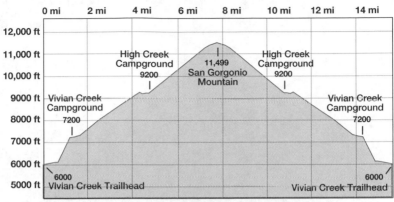

TRAIL 47 San Gorgonio Mountain Elevation Profile

🚶 MILESTONES

▶1 0.0 From Vivian Creek Trailhead, follow dirt road uphill

▶2 0.6 Road ends; trails swings left across Mill Creek wash

▶3 0.7 Find foot of Vivian Creek Trail and ascend steeply

▶4 1.2 Join Vivian Creek; pass Vivian Creek campground

▶5 2.5 Pass Halfway campground

▶6 4.8 Arrive at High Creek campground

▶7 7.2 Junction with San Bernardino Peak Divide Trail; turn right

▶8 7.4 Sky High Trail intersects on the right; keep straight

▶9 7.8 Arrive at San Gorgonio Mountain summit; return by same route

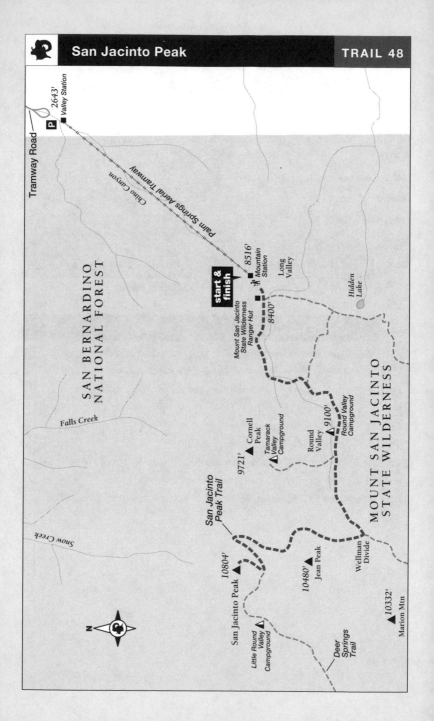

Tramway Road

2643'
Valley Station

P

Chino Canyon

Palm Springs Aerial Tramway

SAN BERNARDINO
NATIONAL FOREST

Falls Creek

Snow Creek

8516'
Mountain
Station

Long
Valley

Hidden
Lake

start &
finish

8400'

Mount San Jacinto State Wilderness
Ranger Hut

9721'
Cornell
Peak

Tamarack
Valley
Campground

9100'

Round
Valley

Round Valley
Campground

MOUNT SAN JACINTO
STATE WILDERNESS

San Jacinto Peak Trail

10804'
San Jacinto Peak

10480'
Jean Peak

Wellman
Divide

10332'
Marion Mtn

Little Round
Valley
Campground

Deer
Springs
Trail

N

San Jacinto Peak

The north face of San Jacinto Peak, at one point soaring 9000 feet up in four horizontal miles, is one of the most imposing escarpments in the U.S. Upon witnessing sunrise on the peak a century ago, John Muir exclaimed, "The view from San Jacinto is the most sublime spectacle to be found anywhere on this earth!" Perhaps Muir was exaggerating—especially after seeing so many high places in California—but the emotion and exhilaration behind his statement is easily understood. Today, there's no great hardship involved in reaching the 10,804-foot summit. Simply take the Palm Springs Aerial Tramway to the trailhead, just 2300 feet in elevation below the peak, and follow well-graded trails all the way up to the top. The ten-minute ascent on the tramway gives you virtually no time to adjust to the high elevation at the start, so to acclimatize you might consider hiking other areas at altitude before tackling this trip.

Best Time

Severe weather can visit San Jacinto Peak, with winter storms bearing down as late as April. By May, most or all of the snow is gone. Around December, the upper elevations of San Jacinto again become the domain of snowshoe and cross-country ski travelers.

Finding the Trail From Highway 111 just
north of Palm Springs, turn west on Tramway Road and continue to the valley station of the Palm Springs Aerial Tramway. Purchase a round-trip

TRAIL USE
Hike, Run
LENGTH
11 miles, 6 hours
ELEVATION GAIN/LOSS
2600'/2600'
DIFFICULTY
– 1 2 3 **4** 5 +
TRAIL TYPE
Out & Back
SURFACE TYPE
Dirt

FEATURES
Mountain
Summit
Autumn Colors
Birds
Great Views
Photo Opportunity
Camping

Great View

ticket there and ride the tram to the mountain station, which includes a lounge and a gift shop. Call the Palm Springs Aerial Tramway, (760) 325-1391, for information and operating hours. The tramway may close for a period in August for maintenance; otherwise, it normally operates 7 days a week year-round.

Trail Description

Start your hike on a paved pathway▶1 leading 0.2 mile downhill from the mountain station to the **Mount San Jacinto State Wilderness** ranger hut▶2 in **Long Valley**. You must obtain a wilderness permit there for travel beyond Long Valley. If the ranger hut is closed, self-registering permits can be obtained outside.

From the ranger hut, follow the wide trail leading steadily uphill for 2 miles to **Round Valley** ▶3—mostly through a coniferous forest of Jeffrey pine, sugar pine, and white fir. Backpacking campsites are located in the Round Valley area and at **Tamarack Valley**, 0.5 mile north of Round Valley via a side trail. Continue your ascent, somewhat steeper now, through thinning lodgepole pines to a trail junction at **Wellman Divide**,▶4 3.2 miles from the start. This is where you get your first impressive view—south over tree-covered summits, foothills, and distant desert and coastal valleys.

After an almost obligatory (common, anyway)

Exploring Further

OPTIONS

Perhaps this "easy" introduction to Southern California's highest elevations will whet your appetite for more lengthy routes in the San Jacinto Mountains. Several other, more challenging routes to San Jacinto Peak originate near Idyllwild, a piney resort community at about 5000 feet elevation, south of the peak.

water or snack break at Wellman Divide, continue your leisurely uphill grind toward **San Jacinto Peak**. You traverse north for more than a mile across a boulder-strewn slope covered by scattered lodge-pole pines and a carpet of low-growing alpine shrubs. Abruptly, you change direction at a switch-back corner, climb southwest for a while, and arrive (2 miles from Wellman Divide) in a saddle just south of the peak itself. ▶5 Veer right, follow the path up along the right (east) side of the summit, pass a stone hut, then scramble from boulder to boulder for a couple of minutes to reach the top. ▶6

The bald, gray (or white if covered by snow) ridge to the north is 11,499-foot **San Gorgonio Mountain** in the San Bernardino Mountains. The Pacific Ocean can sometimes be seen over many miles of coastal haze to the west. Eastward, where the air is usually most transparent, the tan and brown landscape of the desert rolls interminably toward a horizon near Arizona.

Make sure that you leave the summit of San Jacinto Peak in time to get aboard the last downhill tram ride.

Hopefully the weather on San Jacinto's summit will allow you to rest a spell in the warm sun, cupped amid the jumbo-sized rocks, and savor the lightheaded sensation of being on top of the world.

 ▲ Summit

🚶 MILESTONES

▶1	0.0	From tramway station descend on paved path
▶2	0.2	Visit ranger hut; obtain wilderness permit
▶3	2.2	In Round Valley; pass trail to Tamarack Valley on the right
▶4	3.2	Reach Wellman Divide; trail branching south descends to Idyllwild; keep climbing
▶5	5.2	Arrive at junction south of peak, turn north on spur trail toward peak
▶6	5.5	Arrive on San Jacinto Peak summit; return by same route

Appendix

Major Public Agencies

Santa Monica Mountains National Recreation Area
(a unit of the National Park Service dedicated to preserving open space and facilitating recreational use in the Santa Monica Mountains)
401 W. Hillcrest Dr.
Thousand Oaks, CA 91360
(805) 370-2301
www.nps.gov/samo/

Santa Monica Mountains Conservancy
(a state-funded agency that acquires property for public open space and manages parkland in the Santa Monica Mountains/Rim of the Valley areas)
2600 Franklin Canyon Dr.
Beverly Hills, CA 90210
(310) 858-7272
http://ceres.ca.gov/smmc/

Angeles National Forest
(encompasses nearly all of the San Gabriel Mountains)
701 N. Santa Anita Ave.
Arcadia, CA 91006
(626) 574-1613
www.fs.fed.us/r5/angeles/

San Bernardino National Forest
(encompasses the San Bernardino and San Jacinto mountains,
and the easternmost San Gabriel Mountains)
1824 S. Commercenter Cir.
San Bernardino, CA 92408
(909) 382-2600
www.fs.fed.us/r5/sanbernardino/

Cleveland National Forest
(encompasses the Santa Ana Mountains, plus certain mountainous sections
of San Diego County)
10845 Rancho Bernardo Dr., Ste 200
San Diego, CA 92127
(858) 673-6180
www.fs.fed.us/r5/cleveland/

County of Los Angeles Department of Parks and Recreation
(manages park land throughout Los Angeles County)
433 S. Vermont Ave.
Los Angeles, CA 90020
(213) 738-2951
http://parks.co.la.ca.us/

County of Orange Harbors, Beaches & Parks
(manages park land throughout Orange County)
1 Irvine Park Road
Orange, CA 92869
(866) 627-2757
www.ocparks.com/

Index

Sostomo Trail 61
South Mount Hawkins lookout 167
Split Rock 76
Star Rise trail 230
Stone Canyon, Trail 128
Stonyvale 128
Stonyvale Picnic Area 127
Stunt High Trail 53
Sturtevant Falls 147
Sulphur Springs 98, 99
Sunset Ridge fire road
        135-36, 137, 141, 143
Sunset Ridge Trail 136, 137
Swan Rock 183
Swinnerton, Jimmy 166

Tamarack Valley 256
Tapia Park 57
Tapia Spur Trail 57
Teddy's Outpost Picnic Area 132
Telegraph Canyon 201-03
Telegraph Canyon Trail 202
Temescal Canyon 39-40
Temescal Canyon, Trail 40
Temescal Gateway Park 39
Temescal Ridge Trail 39-40
Tepee Outlook 94
Three T's Trail 187
Tom Lucas Trail Camp 124
Topanga State Park 18, 47, 49
Towsley Canyon 106
Trail Canyon 123-24
Trail Canyon Trail 123-24
Trans-Preserve Trail 234, 235
Trippet Ranch 47
Tropical Terrace 59, 60

Upper Winter Creek Trail 147

Vancouver, George 69
Vernal Pool Trail 234
Vetter Mountain 157-58
Vetter Mountain Trail 159
Vincent Gap 169, 170
Vivian Creek 251

Vivian Creek Trail 249, 251
Vogel Flat Picnic Area 127

Walker, Frank 111
Walowski, Joseph 164
water (sources and purity) 12-13
Wellman Divide 256
West Fork National Recreation Trail
        177-179
West Fork San Gabriel River 177-179
West Ridge Trail 230
Westward Beach 67
White City 140
Whiting Ranch Wilderness Park
221-223
Wilacre Park 31-32
wildflowers
        (of the Los Angeles region) 5-6
wildlife (of the Los Angeles region) 3-4
Wildwood Nature Center 95
Wildwood Park 93-95
Will Rogers State Historic Park 35-36
Willow Canyon Road 218
Winter Creek 145, 146

Ye Alpine Tavern 139, 142

Zuma Canyon 71-73
Zuma Ridge Trail 72

Author and Editor

Jerry Schad

Jerry Schad's several parallel careers have encompassed interests ranging from astronomy and teaching to photography and writing. He teaches astronomy and physical science at San Diego Mesa College, and currently chairs the Physical Sciences Department there.

Schad is author of Wilderness Press's *Afoot and Afield* hiking guidebooks for Los Angeles, Orange County, and San Diego, as well as *101 Hikes in Southern California*, and *Trail Runner's Guide San Diego*. For *Top Trails Los Angeles*, his 14th book, he traveled north to revisit some his favorite trails in the foothills and mountains of the "City of Angels."

Joe Walowski Top Trails Editor

Joe Walowski's editing career begins with *Top Trails Los Angeles*. By day, Joe is a strategy consultant to magazine publishers. An avid hiker and climber, he has spent many pleasant days on the top trails throughout California. He makes his home in San Francisco.

Joe conceived of the Top Trails series as the definitive sampler of trails, the "must-do" hikes in the most interesting destinations. Feel free to e-mail feedback on Top Trails to joe@highpointpress.com